W9-AQC-573

THE UTOPIAN AESTHETICS OF THREE AFRICAN AMERICAN WOMEN (TONI MORRISON, GLORIA NAYLOR, JULIE DASH)

The Principle of Hope

THE UTOPIAN AESTHETICS OF THREE AFRICAN AMERICAN WOMEN (TONI MORRISON, GLORIA NAYLOR, JULIE DASH)

The Principle of Hope

Heike Raphael-Hernandez

With a Preface by
Dieter Schulz

The Edwin Mellen Press
Lewiston•Queenston•Lampeter

Library of Congress Cataloging-in-Publication Data

Raphael-Hernandez, Heike
The utopian aesthetics of three African American women (Toni Morrison, Gloria Naylor, Julie Dash) : the principle of hope / Heike Raphael-Hernandez ; with a [preface] by Dieter Schulz.
p. cm.
Includes bibliographical references and index.
ISBN-13: 978-0-7734-4936-7
ISBN-10: 0-7734-4936-1
1. American fiction--African American authors--History and criticism. 2. American fiction--Women authors--History and criticism. 3. Morrison, Toni-Aesthetics. 4. Naylor, Gloria--Aesthetics. 5. Dash, Julie--Aesthetics. 6. Hope in literature. 7. Aesthetics in literature. I. Title.
PS153.N5R37 2008
810.9'9287'08996073--dc22

2008040671

hors série.

A CIP catalog record for this book is available from the British Library.

The Edwin Mellen Press
Box 450
Lewiston, New York
USA 14092-0450

The Edwin Mellen Press
Box 67
Queenston, Ontario
CANADA L0S 1L0

The Edwin Mellen Press, Ltd.
Lampeter, Ceredigion, Wales
UNITED KINGDOM SA48 8LT

Printed in the United States of America

In loving memory

of my father

Hans Günther Sachse

1931 - 2007

Table of Contents

Preface

Starting around the late 1970s, African American women's fiction has been characterized by a remarkable shift in mood: The victimized, broken protagonists of such writers as Nella Larsen and Ann Petry have given way to an array of Black women characters who, however tentatively, manage to overcome the trauma inflicted by racist and sexist abuse. Alice Walker, Toni Morrison, Gloria Naylor, Paule Marshall, Gayl Jones, Ntozake Shange, and other major novelists project images of heroines who move beyond suffering and despair to healing, insight, and partial acceptance--to a vision of regeneration that reaches beyond the individual to include the hope for a renovated and more humane society.

Critics have recognized in these works such familiar patterns as the novel of initiation and the *Bildungsroman*; American Studies scholars may feel tempted to suspect that African American women's fiction has finally linked up with the American Dream. After all, the notion of individual rebirth and renewal in a new, "utopian" framework has been one of the hallmarks of the idea of America ever since the Pilgrim Fathers stepped ashore on Plymouth Rock. Tempting and legitimate as such assessments may be, the problem with generalizations like these is that they provide few criteria for the analysis of specific phenomena. What have we gained by placing Toni Cade Bambara or Bebe More Campbell within the tradition of the American Dream?

The present study offers a fresh look at the utopian element that has always been recognized as a defining feature of the American intellectual tradition. Drawing on Ernst Bloch's *The Principle of Hope* (first published in 1959), the most influential twentieth-century European philosophy of utopian thought, Heike Raphael-Hernandez develops a set of concepts that sheds considerable light on one of the most conspicuous trends in contemporary Black women's writing. According to Bloch, the "utopian impulse" is not confined to the genre of utopia proper; in fact, classic versions of the genre--notably Plato's *Republic* and Thomas More's *Utopia*--tend to freeze the creative potential of this impulse by projecting highly elaborate but static systems of social and political organization. The utopian impulse according to Bloch, in contrast, liberates our urge for a tentative, ongoing, and open-ended process of renewal that encompasses the individual and society alike. From this perspective, the healing and self-empowerment envisaged by African American women novelists manages to elude the tendency for stasis and closure built into traditional "abstract" utopias. Instead, along with the protagonists of the novels, we are offered concrete fragments and glimpses of an interim state of becoming, intimations of an imaginative surplus that promises to break the stranglehold of a status quo characterized by paralysis and death-in-life.

Loosely affiliated with but for decades overshadowed by the Frankfurt School, Ernst Bloch has come to be recognized as one of the most original minds of the twentieth century. Much more accessible than, say, the writings of Adorno or Habermas--not to mention French structuralism and poststructuralism--*The Philosophy of Hope* is informed by a profound appreciation of literature and the fine arts. It comes hardly as a surprise, then, that the analytic concepts of Bloch's *magnum opus* should lend themselves to the discourse of literary criticism. What *is* surprising, though, is the range and the depth of the insights offered into recent Black women's fiction in the present study. Far from forcing an extraneous, "foreign" point of view onto the American scene, Raphael-Hernandez's book offers an example of transatlantic criticism at its best. Coming as they do from a philosophy steeped in Hegel and Marx, Bloch's criteria--perhaps *because* of their apparent distance from things American--provide a set of critical tools that serve these writers in ways that are often unexpected and invariably rewarding.

Dieter Schulz
Professor of English
Chair, American Studies
University of Heidelberg, Germany

Acknowledgments

Many people showed their genuine interest in the fundamental ideas of this project and participated with challenging discussions at many different sites and occasions. I owe thanks to all of them. Because it is not possible to include all, I would like to name some in particular whose ideas contributed to the final product in very different but wonderful ways. The project grew out of my dissertation, for which I was fortunate to have the guidance of Dieter Schultz, who kept encouraging me to, actually insisting, that I turn an idea into reality. Likewise, I also learned much from Dietmar Schloss, one of the other members of my committee. I am also grateful for the valuable insight offered in the early stages of this study by Howard Hastings, Heide Weidner, Jennifer Burden, and Sylvia Meyer.

Major part of the research for this project was done during a one-year stay at Harvard's African American Studies Department. I was fortunate to be part of such a supportive environment, and my thanks go to Henry Louis Gates, Jr., and to Anthony Appiah.

In writing this book, I was extremely privileged to be part of an academic women's research group. Dorothea Fischer-Hornung, Tobe Levin, Alison Goeller, and Monika Müller have provided encouragement, sound advice, and lots of friendship over the years.

Sabine Broeck, Bill Mullen, and Jennifer Herrin read the final manuscript. I would like to thank them for their insightful and wonderful comments and suggestions. I also would like to express my appreciation to Herbert Richardson and Patricia Schultz with whom I had the privilege to work at the Edwin Mellen Press.

My biggest thanks goes to my homefront—Don and Markus, Jakob, and Jonathan—an incredible bunch full of humor, support, and love. That this project is realized is also due to them.

The book is dedicated to my father, Hans Günther Sachse, who shared his tremendous love of books with his children already when we were just in our toddler shoes and who kept nurturing my own fascination with books. Himself a published author, he was always interested in my projects. He died during the time when I was finishing the manuscript for this book. My loving thanks belong to him.

Information about front cover photograph:

The picture shows one of the coaling women who carried coal mined in Europe on and off the steamships in St. Thomas. The photo was used as a postcard in the 1880s.

Permissions

Bailey's Café by Gloria Naylor: Copyright © 1992 by Gloria Naylor. Excerpts reprinted by permission of Houghton Mifflin Harcourt Publishing Company.

Bailey's Café by Gloria Naylor: © 1992 by Gloria Naylor. Reprinted by permission of SLL/Sterling Lord Literistic, Inc. for the publication in the English language in the following territories: Nonexclusive, World, excluding USA and Canada.

Beloved by Toni Morrison: Copyright © 1987 by Toni Morrison. Used by permission of Alfred A. Knopf, a division of Random House, Inc.

Beloved by Toni Morrison: Reprinted by permission of International Creative Management, Inc. Copyright © as provided by Random House. The rights granted herein apply to publication in the English language in the UK and British Commonwealth.

Daughters of the Dust by Julie Dash: Excerpts reprinted with permission by The New Press.

Dessa Rose by Sherley Anne Williams: Copyright © 1986 by Sherley Anne Williams. Reprinted by permission of HarperCollins Publishers.

Dessa Rose by Sherley Anne Williams: Copyright © 1986 by Sherley Anne Williams. Reprinted by permission for the territories of UK and British Commonwealth of Virago Press, an imprint of Little, Brown Book Group, UK.

Jazz by Toni Morrison: Copyright © 1992 by Toni Morrison. Used by permission of Alfred A. Knopf, a division of Random House, Inc.

Jazz by Toni Morrison: Reprinted by permission of International Creative Management, Inc. Copyright © as provided by Random House. The rights granted

Introduction

Dreaming for Empowerment

In her novel *The Color Purple*, Alice Walker introduces her protagonist Celie as a victim of incest, wife abuse, and mental mistreatment. Initially, the combination of these experiences causes Celie to consider herself an absolutely worthless human being. During the course of the novel, however, Walker takes Celie on a journey that leads to Celie's mental and spiritual healing and, additionally, transforms her community into a better place for everyone.

If one considers the tremendous problems the protagonist had to work through and the obstacles she had to overcome, Walker's conclusion resembles a fairy tale ending: finally, everybody comes home after a long and dangerous trip, everybody is happy, and everybody loves everybody else. However, instead of calling Walker's text a modern, perhaps even shallow, fairy tale, I want to argue that it should be read as a concrete utopia according to the theory presented by the German philosopher Ernst Bloch. He outlines his theory in his major work *The Principle of Hope*. Bloch claims that concrete utopian texts are able to make the reader think critically about his or her own individual circumstances. Yet he argues that only when people become consciously aware of the dialectical tendencies in concrete utopias will they recognize the possibilities first for their own personal empowerment and then for their communities. As a result of their conscious awareness, readers will be able to perceive the visions of the texts and will begin to actively dream of becoming agents for change themselves. The notion of the reader's consciously growing awareness of his or her own agency embodies a theory of hope in these concrete utopias. Bloch calls this concept the principle of hope.

Concerning my thesis, *The Color Purple* serves here merely as the prototype for my main argument. I claim that most texts by contemporary African American women writers who have published since the 1970s provide concrete utopian visions. I observe Blochian utopian features in the novels of such diverse writers as Alice Walker, Toni Cade Bambara, Gloria Naylor, Ntozake Shange, Toni Morrison, Gayl Jones, Paule Marshall, Sherley Anne Williams, Bebe Moore Campbell, and Terry McMillan, just to name the major ones.[1] All these authors fulfill Bloch's main requirements for concrete utopias: they send their protagonists on spiritual journeys from broken to healed personalities and, additionally, show how the transformed protagonists catalyze their communities into making progressive changes. I claim that an application of Bloch's theory to contemporary African American women writers enriches a reading of their texts. Citing the African American theorist Cheryl Wall, who argues, "…by reading black women's writing in the context of African and European philosophical and

---

[1] Some scholars could argue that to apply the term "contemporary" to such a large group of writers might not be without problems as the period I am covering—writers who have published since the 1970s—embodies several generations of writers by now. Indeed, one can see attempts to find a distinguishing terminology for these writers. Valerie Lee, for example, distinguishes between "literature of the second Renaissance" and "literature from the new millennium" in her anthology. See Valerie Lee, ed., *The Prentice Hall Anthology of African American Women's Writers* (Upper Saddle River, NJ: Pearson, 2006). And Shelley Reid calls writers such as Bebe Moore Campbell and Terry McMillan contemporary Black women writers beyond Morrison and Walker. See Shelley E. Reid, "Beyond Morrison and Walker: Looking Good and Looking forward in Contemporary Black Women Stories," *African American Review* 34.2 (2000): 313-328. Yet to distinguish the group of writers I will discuss from those authors writing before the 1970s, I have chosen to stay with the term "contemporary," a term still commonly used in current scholarship.

religious systems, we may mark when and how this writing privileges 'other' ways of knowing,"[2] I want to propose that reading contemporary African American women authors' texts in the light of Bloch's concrete utopian theory offers such an "other way of knowing."

Bloch's concrete utopias should not be confused with traditional literary utopias because concrete utopias do not use the narrative devices that characterize the texts of the traditional utopian genre such as Thomas More's classical *Utopia* (1516), Charlotte Perkins Gilman's *Herland* (1915), or Ernest Callenbach's *Ecotopia* (1975). Traditional utopias construct a perfect society, which can be found either on a remote island or planet or even somewhere in the future, and readers learn from this place through the reported observations of a nonutopian traveler. Most of the time, the outsider simply describes a few of the governmental and economic structures of the place.

Yet texts that can be called concrete utopias according to Bloch's theory are not interested in depicting a perfect place but focus rather on the protagonist's spiritual journey from a broken to a healed personality. The spiritual journey contains the *utopian impulse*, as Bloch calls it. The *utopian impulse* is supposed to inspire the reader, who observes an initially struggling and finally succeeding protagonist, toward agency for his or her own circumstances. The setting in concrete utopias often takes place in normal, very real everyday communities that do not imply anything fantastic, remote, or futuristic. In her analysis of Bloch's theory, Angelika Bammer explains the political intention of concrete utopian texts:

> …the utopian gesture is not substitute but transformative, not a movement away, but rather the ability to move within and against existing structures. The utopian … is a constant process of reworking the very cultural scripts into which we not only are written ourselves, but which we participate in

---

[2] Cheryl Wall, ed., Introduction, *Changing Our Own Words. Essays on Criticism, Theory, and Writing by Black Women* (New Brunswick and London: Rutgers University Press, 1989) 9.

> writing. ...the idea of "a utopia" as something fixed [is replaced] with the idea of "the utopian" as an *approach toward*, a movement beyond set limits into the realm of the not-yet-set. At the same time ... the notion of the utopian as unreal [is countered by] the proposition that the utopian is powerfully real in the sense that hope and desire [and even fantasies] are real, never "merely" fantasy. It is a force that moves and shapes history.[3]

Bammer is able to claim concrete utopias as a force that shapes history because Bloch's theory embodies the belief that art is able to motivate people toward personal agency. Bloch's idea of art's motivational ability implies that people's simple longing for a better place can be transformed into progressive politics.

Analyzing the relevance of Bloch's theory for contemporary society, the German sociologist Andreas Maucher argues that an identification with concrete utopias will motivate individuals to change society from below.[4] Consequently, Bloch can also be called *the* philosopher of grassroots movements, and concrete utopian texts can be viewed as grassroots literature.[5]

Regarding contemporary women writers in general, a reading of their texts in connection to Bloch's theory seems to be especially fitting. I base my claim on the fact that later feminism and Bloch's theory share several major premises: As Bammer points out, feminists of the late 1970s insisted in regard to the utopian that "utopia is not to be found in a particular place or form, but rather that it is a

---

[3] Angelika Bammer, *Partial Visions. Feminism and Utopianism in the 1970s* (New York and London: Routledge, 1991) 3.

[4] Andreas Maucher, *Die Rettung des Fortschritts. Ernst Bloch im 'Diskurs der Moderne'* (Konstanz: Hartung-Gorre, 1989) 129.

[5] Concerning the connection between the inspirational power of literature and Ernst Bloch's concrete utopian theory, Verena Kirchner offers in her *Im Bann der Utopie* (Heidelberg: Universitätsverlag C. Winter, 2002) an analysis of several former East German writers and their texts. Although her analysis does have its compelling aspects, her text is not without major problems. As Peter Morris-Keitel points out in his review, Kirchner's reading of Bloch and East German texts is heavily influenced by the "spirit of [Theodor] Adorno," who denounced Bloch's utopian theory (see Peter Morris-Keitel, Rev. of *Im Bann der Utopie*, by Verena Kirchner, *Utopian Studies* 15.1 (2004): 131). Therefore, Kirchner's reading often jumps between regarding Bloch as a truly aesthetically inspirational influence on the one hand, and declaring East German writers as supporters of the totalitarianism of their own society on the other hand.

movement toward possibilities."[6] The German feminist theorist Gabriele Dietze, for example, claims that utopia "is not the place, but the journey."[7]

As I already showed above, the image of the journey is one of Bloch's main theoretical ideas as well. He demands that people should understand that they have to constantly strive to overcome specific historical, cultural, and social forms of oppression because the oppression-free society, the ultimate, perfect place, is only a theoretical, intellectual construction because humans will always exercise some form of oppression. Even if they overcome old forms, they will create new forms. Therefore, people have to learn that they must work constantly on improving their own, respective societies. People who are consciously aware of the necessity of the constant journey and have accepted the fact that revolution cannot happen as one isolated incident in history but must be repeated on a daily basis live with an attitude that Bloch calls the *anticipatory illumination* of the *not-yet.* Such an attitude will lead to hope and spiritual healing, two key aspects of Bloch's theory. As Bammer claims about the importance of the *anticipatory illumination* of the *not-yet* for feminist texts, utopia becomes for Bloch "not just a literary fantasy or philosophical speculation, but a means of spiritual survival."[8]

---

[6] Bammer, *Partial Visions*, 58. In *Partial Visions*, Bammer emphasizes the opportunities Bloch's utopian impulse offers to feminist texts. Although she points in one of her footnotes to the fact that for a long time the relationship between Bloch and feminists has rather "been vexed [because] Bloch himself had little to say about feminism, and feminists, in turn, have had little to say about Bloch," (169) she still argues that Bloch's theory of the *utopian impulse* and of personal agency has so much to offer to feminism that it is time for feminists to explore Bloch's theory, too. For my argument here, I refer solely to Bammer's study because until now she is the only literary critic who has written in detail about the connection between Bloch's concrete utopian theory and feminism/utopianism. Although many studies exist on feminism and utopianism, they all limit their discussions more or less to the traditional utopian genre. See, for example, Ruby Rohrlich and Elaine Hoffman Baruch, eds., *Women in Search of Utopia. Mavericks and Mythmakers* (New York: Schocken Books, 1984), and Mario Klarer, *Frau und Utopie. Feministische Literaturtheorie und Utopischer Diskurs im Anglo-Amerikanischen Roman* (Darmstadt: Wissenschaftliche Buchgesellschaft, 1993).

[7] Gabriele Dietze, *Die Überwindung der Sprachlosigkeit. Texte aus der Neuen Frauenbewegung* (Darmstadt/Neuwied: Luchterhand, 1979) 18.

[8] Bammer, *Partial Visions*, 2.

Many theorists have pointed in general, without reference to Bloch, to the hope and healing content in contemporary Black women writers' texts. For example, in comparison with earlier African American women's texts from the Harlem Renaissance, the Naturalist and Modernist periods, or the Black Arts Movement, contemporary texts allow struggling protagonists not only to recognize negative circumstances but to find the mental and spiritual power within themselves to change those circumstances. Cheryl Wall points out that the protagonists of contemporary texts partake in a mood of righteous anger and triumphant struggle that enables them to move from victim to survivor. According to her, contemporary characters define and "position themselves respectively as potential and active agents of social change."[9] With their specific emphasis on hope and healing, these contemporary texts are very much in line with Bloch's theory.

The move from victim to survivor in contemporary African American women authors' texts is often connected to a process of spiritual awakening. In this regard, the texts meet Bloch's requirement of the psychological journey. Deborah McDowell emphasizes that the psychological journey motif represents a major modifier for these texts:

> Though one can also find the [journey] motif in the works of Black male writers, they do not use it in the same way as do Black female writers. For example, the journey of the Black male character in works by Black men takes him underground.... It is primarily political and social in its implications.... The Black female's journey, on the other hand, though at times touching the political and social, is basically a personal and psychological journey.[10]

---

[9] Wall, Introduction, *Changing Our Own Words*, 3.

[10] Deborah E. McDowell, "New Directions for Black Feminist Criticism," (1980), *Within the Circle. An Anthology of African American Literary Criticism from the Harlem Renaissance to the Present*, ed. Angelyn Mitchell (Durham and London: Duke University Press, 1994) 437.

For Bloch, the image of the psychological journey—the protagonist's growing awareness of his or her own spiritual powers and agency—is essential in the process of empowerment. Yet since Bloch is a philosopher and not a psychologist, he is not interested in the protagonist's spiritual journey per se. For him, the spiritual healing process has to serve a higher purpose: He wants people who have experienced the growing awareness of self-empowerment to become active in their respective communities. On the one hand, they should work on progressive changes themselves, and, on the other hand, they should influence others toward societal improvements. The notion of the protagonist's community change represents one of the key ideas in Bloch's theory, for it is here that the text will inspire the reader toward personal agency in his or her own society.

The contemporary Black women writers' texts meet Bloch in this regard, too. Their initially struggling and finally succeeding protagonists all improve, more or less, their immediate surroundings or at least start with the help of their spiritual attitudes to work on improvements so that the reader can imagine how a possible future in these fictitious communities would look like. Sandi Russell explains about Alice Walker's texts, for example, that the "move from loss to hope" causes the protagonists to participate in the "transformation of society."[11] Joanne V. Gabbin, too, observes the protagonists' active participation in societal changes in these texts. She claims that because of an "unabashed confrontation with the past and [a] clear-eyed vision of the future," the texts move from "protest toward revelation and informed social change."[12]

---

[11] Sandi Russell, "The Silenced Speak," *Render Me My Song. African-American Women Writers from Slavery to the Present* (New York: St. Martin's Press, 1990) 122.

[12] Joanne V. Gabbin, "A Laying On of Hands: Black Women Writers Exploring the Roots of Their Folk and Cultural Tradition," *Wild Women in the Whirlwind. Afra-American Culture and the Contemporary Literary Renaissance*, eds. Joanne M. Braxton and Andree Nicola McLaughlin (New Brunswick: Rutgers University Press, 1990) 249.

Since I apply the theory of a German Jewish male philosopher, who is not even a contemporary of the current African American women authors, to these writers' texts, I have to address a concern often heard in the discourse of Black critics. Black feminist scholars have often pointed to the problem of applying critical theories of Western men to texts by Black women authors. Oppositional voices such as Barbara Christian's or Deborah McDowell's are concerned because they see that the abstract, rational models of theorists such as Ferdinand de Saussure, Louis Althusser, Jacques Lacan, and Jacques Derrida speak about the human experience in such a general way that they do not allow for any space for the specific experiences or emotions of African American women in their particular historical and social settings.[13] Likewise, Mae Henderson criticizes the fact that many scholars and theorists draw on paradigms that are "not grounded in African American history and culture. …such a theoretical move risks appropriating the geographically and historically specific experiences of African Americans to the theoretical exigencies of a non-African American constituency."[14]

Even in regard to feminist theories, Christian cautions, "Seldom do feminist theorists take into account the complexity of life—that women are of many races and ethnic backgrounds with different histories and cultures and that as a rule women belong to different classes that have different concerns."[15] In

---

[13] See especially Barbara Christian's two essays "The Race for Theory" and "But What Do We Think We're Doing Anyway: The State of Black Feminist Criticism(s) or My Version of a Little Bit of History," both in *Within the Circle. An Anthology of African American Literary Criticism from the Harlem Renaissance to the Present*, ed. Angelyn Mitchell (Durham and London: Duke University Press, 1994) 348-359 and 499-514. In addition, see also Deborah E. McDowell's "Transferences: Black Feminist Thinking: The 'Practice' of 'Theory,'" *The Changing Same. Black Women's Literature, Criticism, and Theory* (Bloomington and Indianapolis: Indiana University Press, 1995) 156-176.

[14] Mae Henderson, "'Where, by the Way, Is this Train Going?': A Case for Black (Cultural) Studies," *Postcolonial Theory and the United States. Race, Ethnicity, and Literature*, eds. Amritjit Singh and Peter Schmidt (Jackson: University Press of Mississippi, 2000) 98.

[15] Christian, "The Race for Theory," 355.

addition to cautioning against lumping African American women's experiences into simply either a universal human or a general female experience, several Black feminist critics are concerned about the often ignored fact that the "experience of Afro-American women is unmistakably polyvalent."[16] If this fact is ignored by critics, Mae Henderson, for example, sees the danger that the assumption of an internal Black woman identity may automatically lead to a "simple and reductive paradigm of otherness"[17] that disregards the fact that even Black women themselves belong to different classes, cultures, and historical settings.

Yet all these oppositional voices do not intend to denounce the connection between critical theories and African American women writers but rather want to warn against applications that do not take the specifics of Black women's lives into consideration. Mae Henderson suggests that if a critic regards the fact that every African American woman's text speaks from a "multiple and complex social, historical, and cultural positionality," it is possible to constitute "a dialogue of difference [in regard to] a complex black female subjectivity."[18] If one pays attention to these specific points, then several critics encourage an application of literary theories to African American texts.[19] In her discussion of Black women writings in connection to theory, Cheryl Wall, for example, even suggests

---

[16] Wall, Introduction, *Changing Our Own Words*, 10.

[17] Mae Henderson, "Speaking in Tongues: Dialogics, Dialectics, and the Black Woman Writer's Literary Tradition," *Changing Our Own Words*, ed. Cheryl Wall (New Brunswick and London: Rutgers University Press, 1989) 17.

[18] Henderson, "Speaking in Tongues, " 19.

[19] For my argument, see especially Deborah E. McDowell, "New Directions for Black Feminist Criticism," (1980), *Within the Circle. An Anthology of African American Literary Criticism from the Harlem Renaissance to the Present*, ed. Angelyn Mitchell (Durham and London: Duke University Press, 1994) and Cheryl Wall's essay collection *Changing Our Own Words.* In Wall's collection, several Black feminist critics such as Mae Henderson, Valerie Smith, Barbara Christian and Deborah E. McDowell apply contemporary literary theories to Black women writers' texts under the specific aspect of the "complex black female subjectivity," (19) thus creating a "dialogue of difference" (19), as Mae Henderson puts it.

considering more relational readings with the help of theory, thus putting individual texts into dialogue with each other. For her, an application of theory would help in the process of locating Black women's writings in their multiple contexts. In line with Barbara Smith,[20] Wall proposes a "simultaneity of discourse"[21] that does not ignore the specifics of race and gender and their interrelationships. Henry Louis Gates, Jr., supports this idea when he argues in his *Figures in Black* that critics of African American literature should not shy away from theory but should "translate it into the black idiom."[22] Likewise, Karla Holloway invites critics to read contemporary African American women writers in "multiplied" ways as the texts' structures themselves are "multiplied"; she explains, "This literature displays the gathered effects of these literary structures to the extent that, when we can identify and recognize them, we are able to specify their relationship to thematic and stylistic emphases of the traditions illustrated in these works."[23]

Bloch's theory indeed allows such an application Henderson asks from theory. His theory would indeed consider the "multiple and complex social, historical, and cultural positionality"[24] of Black women because Bloch himself claims that every work of art and, therefore, every example of literature can deal with only one very specific fragment of the ultimate human hope, but not with the entire human condition in general. He calls this concept *fragments of the ultimate*

---

[20] See her groundbreaking essay on African American women writers and critical theory: Barbara Smith, "Toward a Black Feminist Criticism (1977)," *Within the Circle. An Anthology of African American Literary Criticism from the Harlem Renaissance to the Present*, ed. Angelyn Mitchell (Durham and London: Duke University Press, 1994) 410-427.

[21] Wall, Introduction, *Changing Our Own Words*, 9.

[22] Henry Louis Gates, Jr., *Figures in Black. Words, Signs, and the "Racial" Self* (New York: Oxford University Press, 1987) xxi.

[23] Karla Holloway, "Revision and (Re)membrance: A Theory of Literary Structures in Literature by African-American Women Writers," (1990), *The Prentice Hall Anthology of African American Women's Writers*, ed. Valerie Lee (Upper Saddle River, NJ: Pearson, 2006) 405.

[24] Henderson, "Speaking in Tongues, " 19.

true human identity. Since his concept of fragments, too, asks individuals to consider the specifics of every expression of art in regard to its particular historical and social setting, I claim that it is indeed possible to read contemporary African American women writers' texts through the lens of this European male philosopher.[25]

In my first chapter I will deal with Bloch's concrete utopian theory. First, I will give a detailed analysis of his theory in general; second, I will explain the connection of this theory to literature in particular. The subsequent chapters will apply Bloch's thoughts to specific texts by selected contemporary African American women authors.

As I have discussed above, Black feminist critics such as Henderson and McDowell ask for the consideration of the particular historical, cultural, and social circumstances of every text. Therefore, in chapters 2–4, I will discuss such specific settings. For my discussion, I have chosen Toni Morrison's *Beloved*, Gloria Naylor's *Bailey's Café*, and Julie Dash's *Daughters of the Dust*. Dash's

---

[25] So far, a direct application of Bloch's theory to African American literature has not been done. Yet, Francis Shor uses an approach very similar to mine and applies Bloch's theory of hope to African American history. In her convincing essay, she looks at the Black freedom movement, in particular at the SNCC and their members' struggle for civil rights during the period from 1960 to 1965. Like me, Shor claims that although one cannot detect any direct Blochian influences—nowhere does Stokely Carmichael, for example, claim that he read Bloch and *The Principle of Hope*—one is able to find Bloch's specific utopian aspirations. In light that Bloch sees utopian surplus and revolutionary hope in many different expressions of human activity, Shor accordingly reads the Black freedom movement through Blochian theoretical lenses. See Francis Shor, "Utopian Aspirations in the Black Freedom Movement: SNCC and the Struggle for Civil Rights, 1960-1965," *Utopian Studies* 15.2 (2004): 173-189. Likewise, Shor maintains that Robin D.G. Kelley's scholarship on African American social movements presents a Blochian analysis in its best forms; in her review of Kelley's *Freedom Dreams. The Black Radical Imagination*, she sees Bloch's anticipatory consciousness as deeply embedded "in the alternative visions and oppositional politics covered" (128) in the book's argument. See Francis Shor, Rev. of *Freedom Dreams. The Black Radical Imagination*, by Robin D.G. Kelley, *Utopian Studies* 15.1 (2004): 128-129. Indeed, in his introduction Kelley explains in quite Blochian terms that even the so-called failures of radical social movements should not be seen as failures because "it is precisely those alternative visions and dreams that inspire new generations to continue to struggle for change" (ix). And with this idea, Kelley meets Bloch: Bloch would call Kelley's alternative visions the *utopian surplus*; Kelley uses poet Jayne Cortez's words, "somewhere in advance of nowhere" (xii). See Robin D.G. Kelley, *Freedom Dreams. The Black Radical Imagination* (Boston: Beacon Press, 2002).

work differs from the other in that it is not a novel, but a feature film.[26] I deliberately include a discussion of her film because I want to show that Bloch's theory about dreaming for empowerment works not only with contemporary African American women authors but with the film producers as well. I even think that Bloch's theory is latent in many other expressions of contemporary art by African American women such as poetry, drama, songs, dance, painting, to name just a few. Yet a detailed discussion of every genre in which African American women artists participate would go beyond the scope of my text. Therefore, I have limited my examples to two novels and one film.

In my last chapter I attempt to give a general overview of texts by contemporary African American women writers that contain the Blochian utopian impulse. I will show that although individual works are written for specific situations that differ completely from each other, the texts' combined strength lies in their potential toward encouragement to dream about changed circumstances.

[26] After the success of her film, Julie Dash actually published a novel with the same title, *Daughters of the Dust* (New York: Dutton, 1997). However, the content of her book should not be confused with her film. Her book is rather a continuation of the film's plot because in the novel, Dash starts the book where she ended her film because she follows her film's protagonists, the Peazants, to New York City.

Chapter 1

The Construction of a Concrete Utopian Aesthetic: Concrete Utopian Thoughts in Ernst Bloch's *The Principle of Hope*

Bloch outlines his concrete utopian theory in *The Principle of Hope*. He wrote this monumental work during the 1930s and 1940s at Harvard University while he was in American exile from Nazi Germany.

Before he offers his own concrete utopian theory, he begins his work with a discussion of the shortcomings of the traditional utopian genre. He claims that the traditional literary utopian texts, which he calls social or abstract utopias, represent a failure because they do not encourage readers to change their own conditions in reality. Among the most famous abstract utopias, he counts Plato's *Republic* as the oldest, but also St. Augustine's *City of God*, Francis Bacon's *New Atlantis*, and Sir Thomas More's *Utopia*. According to Bloch, these artificial constructions are unable to offer a true challenge to the dominant system of the reader's historical context because they create abstract, remote societies that are disconnected from our own world and describe only economic and political structures. The individual, however, who hopes for changed, better circumstances for him- or herself does not dream about different governmental structures, but, as Bloch believes, about the "true identity of man who has come to himself with his world successfully achieved for him" (313).[27] Therefore, since the *true identity* represents the foundation for all conscious dreams and hopes, the individual and not governmental structures should become the basis for every constructed attempt of a better future.

Bloch sees another failure of the traditional utopian literary genre in its assumption that a perfect human society might indeed exist one day because the texts depict ultimate perfect circumstances. As Peter Ruppert points out, in traditional utopias "social relations are always harmonious, ethical conflicts are always minimal, everyone we meet, it seems, is always smiling, content and happy."[28]

The idea of the perfect place leads to another weakness of the traditional utopia: its assumption that a change in political and economic structures will cause a change in human character and will consequently produce a new human being. However, these new human beings fail to resemble authentic humans who would be able to experience emotions. Rather, all members of the utopian community represent stereotypes that serve only the purpose of describing a perfect place. Since the authors of traditional utopias are interested only in emphasizing economic and political structures of the utopian society, they fail to bring out the unique hopes and wishes of individuals.

Furthermore, Bloch criticizes the entire system of the utopian community. For instance, because the author considers the society already perfect and consequently does not see any need for development, he or she creates a utopia with absolutely changeless, nondeveloping features. Frank Manuel observes that

---

[27] All references to *The Principle of Hope* in this chapter will be given in parentheses in the text and will be cited from the following edition: Ernst Bloch, *The Principle of Hope*, trans. Neville Plaice, Stephen Plaice, and Paul Knight (Cambridge, MA: The MIT Press, 1986).

[28] Peter Ruppert, *Reader in a Strange Land. The Activity of Reading Literary Utopias* (Athens: University of Georgia Press, 1986) 2.

"most utopias have built-in safeguards against radical alterations of the structures."[29] Bloch criticizes that abstract utopias simply depict the perfect society without describing at all the process and the different steps that led to its perfection in the first place. According to him, however, a reader cannot learn anything from a nonstruggling and nondeveloping community.

In addition, Bloch criticizes the total denial of the possibility of a future descend. He argues:

> In the honest, yet abstract utopias the … belief in progress has very often facilitated the illusion of undisturbed success and advance. Among all the utopians only one, Fourier, has maintained that even in the better future every phase has its ascending line, but also the danger of a descending one. An abstract utopia, even the so-called socialist state of the future … very rarely knows any real danger. (477)

This implies that traditional utopias give readers the illusion that taking care of the utopian society and actively preserving it is no longer necessary.[30]

Bloch believes that the failure of abstract utopias was predetermined as soon as the utopian idea was confined to a literary institution "instead of being perceived and cultivated in the concrete totality of being" (478). Therefore, he rejects abstract utopias and calls for concrete utopias.

In concrete utopias, the utopian thought is not limited anymore to a particular literary genre but can be discovered in any manifestation of a human attempt to combine hope and development; for Bloch, "every work of art, every central philosophy had and has a utopian window in which there lies a landscape which is still developing" (623). He sees developing utopian landscapes in many

---

[29] Frank Manuel, *Utopias and Utopian Thought* (Boston: Houghton Mifflin Company, 1966) 31.

[30] In his analysis of traditional utopias and Bloch's hope concept, Zygmunt Bauman takes a slightly different approach to the dangers of depicting a perfect place. He argues that these utopias do not only deny the possibility of a future descend as Bloch sees it, but in a place that is perfect, it will necessarily happen that "any further change could only be a change for the worse" (64). See Zygmunt Bauman, "To Hope Is Human," *TIKKUN* 19.6 (2004): 64-67.

diverse fields, such as history, technology, architecture, painting, music, dance, ethics, pottery, natural science, medicine, and religion. For example, concerning history, Bloch considers the Peasant Revolt in medieval Germany, the French Revolution, the Paris Commune, the October Revolution in Russia, and all other democratic revolutions to be concrete utopias. Burghart Schmidt points out that Bloch changes the concept of utopia from a literary genre to an attitude: Utopia becomes a "mood of thinking which holds closely to history and reality."[31]

All concrete utopian activities or events contain a *spiritual surplus*. Tom Moylan explains Bloch's idea of the *surplus*: "In each victory of the human project there remains a specific type of hope which is not that of the present and which carries that victorious moment beyond itself, anticipating the next one."[32] This *spiritual surplus*, also called *utopian surplus*, allows a specific event or activity to transcend its particular period and connect with the ultimate universal human ability to strive toward changes. Bloch sees the *utopian surplus* in every field of human creativity. In his text, he explains this idea repeatedly in examples such as the following:

> There is a spirit of utopia in the final predicate of every great statement, in the Strasbourg cathedral and in the Divine Comedy, in the expectant music of Beethoven and in the latencies of the Mass in B minor. It is the despair which still contains an unum necessarium even as something lost, and in the hymn to joy. Kyrie and Credo rise in the concept of utopia as that of comprehended hope in a completely different way, even when the reflection of mere time-bound ideology has been shed, precisely then. (158)

Bloch believes that the past embodies a *cultural inheritance* and that the *utopian surplus* still needs to be extracted from it; this "inheritance that is to be claimed

---

[31] Burghart Schmidt, *Kritik der reinen Utopie. Eine sozialphilosophische Untersuchung* (Stuttgart: Metzler, 1988) 79.

[32] Tom Moylan, "The Locus of Hope: Utopia versus Ideology," *Science-Fiction Studies 9* (1982): 160.

from the past, however, is not a legacy of fixed tradition, but of undischarged hope-content and utopian content in the works of the past."[33]

The *utopian surplus* is closely connected to another concept, the *novum.* The *novum* stands for the "new" aspect in every action and contains the substance that is worth saving for the future. In this regard, Bloch differentiates between *true* and *untrue future*. *Untrue future* includes all acts that will happen in the future as mere repetition of acts that have already happened before: If, for example, a person will get up, have breakfast, and go to work tomorrow, he or she views these events as future today, but they imply *untrue future* because they do not provide any novelty. Only acts that have not happened before can be part of *true future*. The *utopian surplus* is connected with *true future* because it embodies the visions of completely new circumstances that have not existed before in history.

Looking at literature, for Bloch any literature that portrays transforming protagonists or transforming societies contains *utopian surplus* because a society completely free of any oppression is still not part of any historical reality. He argues that literature can be "like a labority [sic!] where events, figures and characters are driven to their typical, characteristic end, to an abysmal or blissful end; this essential vision of characters and situations ... presupposes possibility beyond already exiting reality" (15). Consequently, Bloch allows any literature that contains *utopian surplus* to be called concrete utopian literature.

Bloch claims that the capacity to experience *utopian surplus* is a fundamental human ability because of the existence of an ultimate, finished human essence. Although no one possesses the ultimate essence in its fullest potential because every person is equipped with merely parts of the essence, or with an "unfinished essence,"[34] as David Gross calls it, an individual is able to

---

[33] Neville Plaice, Stephen Plaice, and Paul Knight, Translators' Introduction, *The Principle of Hope*, by Ernst Bloch (Oxford: Basil Blackwell, 1986) xxxvii.

[34] David Gross, "Ernst Bloch and the Dialectics of Hope," *The Unknown Dimension*, eds. Dick Howard and Karl E. Klare (New York: Basic Books, 1972) 107.

sense that this finished, ultimate human essence must exist. This presentiment allows him or her to turn longing into striving. Because of its unfinished essence, the human race is still on its way to becoming what it potentially should be, or, as Bloch describes it, "man is en route" or "underway."[35] George Steiner explains Bloch's idea with the thought that "human beings have just started to be human beings."[36] For the Marxist Bloch, of course, the goal of "man en route" is the transformation of the world into a place without any discrimination or oppression, where human self-realization can reach its fullest potential, where "man is walking upright."[37]

But how does a person know what his or her finished essence, the ultimate being in perfection, should look like so that he or she may be guided during his or her journey? According to Bloch, dreams are able to point to the ultimate human essence. Using dreams as guides, Bloch adds a completely new dimension to philosophy. The novelty of dreams as guides is closely connected to another novelty, the individual's responsibility for the future. Bloch argues, "Not-yet-Conscious, Not-Yet-Become, although it fulfills the meaning of all men and the horizon of all being, has not even broken through as a word, let alone as a concept. This blossoming field lies almost speechless in previous philosophy" (6). Although Karl Marx had already introduced the notion of future-directness into philosophy,[38] he still saw the future as subject to the laws of historical and

---

[35] Plaice, Plaice, and Knight, Translators' Introduction, *The Principle of Hope*, xxxiii.

[36] George Steiner, "Träume nach vorwärts," *Materialien zu Ernst Blochs Prinzip Hoffnung*, ed. Burghart Schmidt, edition suhrkamp 111 (Frankfurt am Main: Suhrkamp, 1978) 196.

[37] Plaice, Plaice, and Knight, Translators' Introduction, *The Principle of Hope*, xxxiii.

[38] All philosophy before Marx is more concerned with analyzing human society and the relationships of humans toward each other. Marx is the one who insists that philosophy has to look ahead. His famous statement, his eleventh thesis on Feuerbach, "Philosophers have only interpreted the world, in various ways; the point, however, is to change it" expresses the novelty of his philosophy.

economic development that the individual is not able to direct or influence. Bloch, on the other hand, adds the individual possibility to philosophy, for he believes that an individual is not just capable of dreaming about the future, but also of getting actively and individually involved in social change. This is precisely the point where he differs from Marx, for Bloch bases his theory on the fundamental dialectical interaction between the subjective and the objective factor in human history. Contrary to Marx, Bloch believes that the individual is the prime mover of history.[39] Bloch emphasizes vehemently the importance of the human agency rooted in individual consciousness because, as Ze'ev Levy explains about Bloch's theory, "utopia can become an objective and real possibility only when it is not bound by predetermined conditions. Only an unconditioned utopia can become a realizable utopia."[40] Hanna Gekle, too, emphasizes that the human as agent is one of Bloch's key terms in his utopian theory because "objective-real possibilities can never happen from alone, but the human being is supposed to function as a catalyst for the positive possibilities and to hinder the negative possibilities."[41]

For this notion of the hope-inspired acting individual, Bloch has always been tremendously criticized, the representatives of the Frankfurt School being among his most outspoken opponents.[42] Theodor Adorno, for example, declared

---

[39] Concerning art and a possible Marxist aesthetic theory, Bloch argued as early as the 1930s against critical realism, which he considered too simple in its aesthetic expression and called it a form of vulgar Marxism. For more details, see Kirchner, *Im Bann der Utopie*, 43-46.

[40] Ze'ev Levy, "Utopia and Reality in the Philosophy of Ernst Bloch," *Utopian Studies* 1.2 (1990): 6.

[41] Hanna Gekle, Afterword, *Abschied von der Utopie? Vorträge*, by Ernst Bloch, ed. Hanna Gekle, edition suhrkamp 104 (Frankfurt am Main: Suhrkamp, 1980) 218.

[42] Bloch had to experience rejection and immense critique of his hope theory at all times after the publication of *The Principle of Hope*. His most famous opponents came from the members of the Frankfurt School. Since a discussion of these differences would go beyond the scope of this work, for more details about the differences between the Frankfurt School members and Bloch himself, see an excellent essay by Adriana S. Benzaquen, "Thought and Utopia in the Writings of Adorno, Horkheimer, and Benjamin," *Utopian Studies* 9.2 (1998): 149-162. See also Roland Bothner, *Die Materie, die Kunst und der Tod. Studien zu Ernst Bloch aus den Jahren 1986 bis 2006* (Heidelberg: Edition Publish & Parish, 2006), and Giuseppe Tassone, "The Politics of

that "hope is not a principle" for philosophy.[43] Yet as the philosopher Zygmunt Bauman pointed out as recently as 2004, philosophy that denies hope as a principle has failed to meet the challenges of the late twentieth and early twenty-first centuries.[44] Bauman recognizes the problem that philosophers such as Theodor Adorno or Jürgen Habermas have had with the term "hope" because this term "acquired in the course of modern history the semantic flavor of a fanciful, perhaps inane pipe-dream and found itself in modern thesauruses in the company of such terms as 'figmental', 'chimerical', 'impractical' or 'dreamy-eyed'."[45] However, Bauman argues that the twenty-first century urgently needs theories such as Bloch's idea of collective hope for the *not-yet-become* because he sees a danger in current society that has not been there before. He claims:

> ...happiness has become a private affair, and a matter of here and now. The happiness of others is no more—or better be no more—a condition of one's own felicity. Each moment of happiness is, after all, lived through in a company that may still be around, but more likely will not be, when the next moment of happiness arrives. Unlike the utopian model of good life, happiness is thought of as an aim to be pursued individually.... In the transgressive imagination of liquid modernity the 'place' (whether physical or social) has been replaced by the unending sequence of new beginnings, inconsequentiality of deeds has been substituted for fixity of order, and the desire of a different today has elbowed out any concern with a better tomorrow.[46]

Likewise, Fredric Jameson sees that philosophy for the twenty-first century has to rethink certain claims, and he argues for the necessity of concepts such as Bloch's

---

Metaphysics: Adorno and Bloch on Utopia and Immortality," *European Legacy* 9.3 (2004): 357-367.

[43] Kirchner, *Im Bann der Utopie*, 43.

[44] Bauman, "To Hope Is Human," 64.

[45] Zygmunt Bauman, "Utopia with No Topos," *History of the Human Sciences* 16.1 (2003): 15.

[46] Bauman, "Utopia with No Topos," 23-24.

because "without them our visions of alternative future and utopian transformations remain politically and existentially inoperative, mere thought experiments and mental games without any visceral commitment."[47]

Again, for Bloch, the realization that both positive and negative possibilities exist in the future and that the hope-inspired individual carries a necessary societal responsibility for change is essential. Since history always has the potential to go the disastrous way, too, the acting human being has to realize that he or she is responsible for both outcomes, and these outcomes will occur because of visions—dreams—he or she has.

The question, of course, that has to be asked and is indeed asked by Bloch is, "How is the most ordinary kind of life, the quiet everyday kind, transformed through dreams?" (31). Contrary to Sigmund Freud, who is interested in night dreams and their revelations about the past, Bloch analyzes daydreams. In regard to his utopian concept, Bloch considers Freud's ideas about night dreams and their relation to the unconscious unimportant for an individual's self-empowerment toward agency.[48] Bloch explains his rejection:

> The unconscious in Freud is therefore one into which something can only be pushed back ... *never a Not-Yet-Conscious*, an element of progressions; it consists rather of regressions. Accordingly, even the process of making this unconscious conscious only clarifies What Has Been; i.e., *there is nothing new in the Freudian unconscious.* (56)

Consequently, Bloch places greater value on daydreams because they embody conscious wishes for a better life. The conscious element, on the other hand,

---

[47] Fredric Jameson, "The Politics of Utopia," *New Left Review* 25 (2004): 53.

[48] The differences between Freud's and Bloch's theories of the subconscious have been the subject of several investigations. See, for example, Hanna Gekle, *Wunsch und Wirklichkeit. Blochs Philosophie des Noch-Nicht-Bewußten und Freuds Theorie des Unbewußten* (Frankfurt am Main: Suhrkamp, 1986). See also Dietmar Heubrock, *Utopie und Lebensstil. Eine empirische Untersuchung zur Bedeutung von Ernst Blochs Konzept der "konkreten Utopie" für eine materialistisch-psychologische Utopieforschung (*Köln: Pahl-Rugenstein, 1988).

allows that the daydream "sketches freely chosen and repeatable figures in the air, it can rant and rave, but also brood and plan" (86). On the other hand, the dreamer's ego remains preserved because it "does not appear in the day dream. On the contrary, it is there very actively and does not exercise any sort of censorship, with the result that wishes function even better in the day dream, more visibly than in the night dream, not disguised, but shameless, uninhibitedly open."[49]

As long as society does not provide perfect conditions, every person will have conscious dreams of unrealized happiness. Yet for Bloch, it is essential to differentiate between two kinds of conscious daydreams. He explains:

> Everybody's life is pervaded by daydreams: one part is just stale, even enervating escapism, even booty for swindlers, but another part is provocative, is not content just to accept the bad which exists, does not accept renunciation. This other part has hoping at its core, and is teachable. It can be extricated from the unregulated daydream and from its sly misuse, can be activated undimmed. (3)

Therefore, he clearly distinguishes between two categories:

(1) the daydream that merely provides an escape from reality but does not enable the dreamer to become active;

(2) the dream that enables the dreamer to work against unsatisfactory circumstances, thereby changing society.

Because the first category represents only an exercise in escapism, it diminishes the ability to envision improved circumstances and nourishes only a nihilistic attitude. Many people remain in the realm of the nihilistic escape dream without ever entering the state of the second category.

The second category, which offers hope, epitomizes the dream that Bloch regards as an important source of utopian imagination. Because the enabling dream looks toward the future, Bloch calls this particular kind of daydream *forward dreaming* (10). He values it highly, for if an individual is *forward*

---

[49] Ernst Bloch, "Man as Possibility," *Cross Currents* (Summer 1968): 273.

dreaming, "the weary, weakening quality that can be characteristic of mere longing then disappears; on the contrary, longing now shows what it can really do … it is capable of revolutionary consciousness, it can climb into the carriage of history" (1365).

In connection with these two different dream categories, Bloch analyzes the different emotions that cause people to experience daydreams. He distinguishes between filled and expectant emotions:

> …filled emotions (like envy, greed, admiration) are those whose drive-intention is short-term, whose drive-object lies ready, if not in individual attainability, then in the already available world. Expectant emotions (like anxiety, fear, hope, belief), on the other hand, are those whose drive-intention is long-term, whose drive-object does not yet lie ready, not just in individual attainability, but also in the already available world, and therefore still occurs in the doubt about exit or entrance. (74)

While filled emotions are connected with the nihilistic escape dream, expectant emotions belong to the enabling dream because they have a greater anticipatory character than filled emotions; i.e., expectant emotions open up entirely to new future possibilities. Because of their anticipatory character, expectant emotions enable humans to turn to agency: Whereas within the old framework, filled emotions would only cause a hungry person to search for food immediately, expectant emotions would seek to change the situation that causes hunger in the first place. Thus, "revolutionary interest" is born (75).

Revolutionary interest enables the individual to get a glimpse of the *not-yet* or *not-yet-become*, another important key concept in Bloch's theory. According to Bloch, every person is equipped with a subconscious ability to anticipate the future. He calls this ability to envision the future, or to get a glimpse of the *not-yet-become*, the *anticipatory illumination* or the *anticipatory consciousness*. The anticipatory ability is closely connected to hope; in this case, "hope is not taken only as emotion, as the opposite of fear … but more essentially as a directing act of a cognitive kind" (12). Because it connects hope with reason, the *anticipatory consciousness* connects the expectant emotions to their utopian function. Bloch explains:

> Only when reason starts to speak, does hope, in which there is no guile, begin to blossom again. The Not-Yet-Conscious itself must become *conscious* in its act, *known* in its content, as the process of dawning, on the one hand, as what is dawning, on the other. And so the point is reached where hope itself ... no longer just appears as a merely self-based feeling ... but in a *conscious-known* way as *utopian function*. (144)

Bloch calls this conscious hope, which knows its ability to change circumstances, the *hope of a knowing kind.* He argues, "... the *act-content* of hope is, as a consciously illuminated, knowingly elucidated content, the *positive utopian function*; the *historical content* of hope, first represented in ideas ... is *human culture referred to its concrete-utopian horizon*" (146). On a cognitive level, hope is the opposite of memory. Remo Bodei explains that Bloch's concept of hope "...is not directed toward an abstract, vague, and distant future, but it is hope directed toward the present and its potentials."[50] As humans, however, we are not able to envision or anticipate the future in its fullest, only in fragments. But even if an individual is allowed only to see fragments of the *not-yet-become*, he or she will still experience the empowering and knowing hope and consequently start to change his or her respective circumstances.

Bloch emphasizes repeatedly that he does not talk about an egocentric hope that has in mind only private gains and advantages. For his theory, he deals with the hope that wants to change the world. Bloch's ultimate goal is the human society in which subject and object no longer face each other as strangers. Virginio Marzocchi emphasizes that although Bloch usually uses the terms "individual," "self-realization," and "subject," he does not have the limited individual's own small desires in mind. Bloch's individual realizes that his or her

---

[50] Remo Bodei, "Darf man noch hoffen?," *Verdinglichung und Utopie. Ernst Bloch und Georg Lukacs zum 100. Geburtstag*, eds. Arno Münster, Michael Löwy, and Nicolas Tertulian (Frankfurt am Main: Sendler, 1987) 214.

own future is inseparably connected to the fate of society at large. According to Marzocchi, Bloch makes it very clear in his later work, *Erbschaft dieser Zeit*, that his subjective factor is not connected to the idealistic character of individual wishes, but to a person's realization and wish for a better and changed society that will be human for everybody.[51]

Bloch himself never developed an aesthetic theory to correspond with his utopian theory. However, as Hans Holländer emphasizes, art philosophy can be found throughout Bloch's work.[52] In his *Principle of Hope*, Bloch explains repeatedly that the appearance of the *not-yet-become* in art has to be considered the major example of *utopian pre-appearance*. According to Burghart Schmidt, Bloch considers art the truest and purest expression of *utopian conscious*, for art is the medium that is able to display *pre-appearance*.[53] Gert Ueding edited a collection of essays by Bloch which Ueding called *Aesthetic of the Pre-Appearance*. In his introduction, Ueding claims that although Bloch never came up with an aesthetic of his own, his texts still allow for the discovery of such an aesthetic.[54]

Bloch is not interested in art as simply depicting reality, but as creating new reality. Peter Brenner explains that with Bloch, since art is not appearance anymore, but *pre-appearance*, it differs now from an illusion because an illusion is removed from reality whereas the foundation of Bloch's *pre-appearance* is

---

[51] Virginio Marzocchi, "Utopie als 'Novum' und 'letzte Wiederholung' bei Ernst Bloch, " *Ernst Bloch. Text und Kritik*, ed. Heinz Ludwig Arnold, special edition (München: edition text + kritik gmbh, 1985) 198.

[52] Hans Holländer, "Der Bildcharakter des 'Vor-Scheins', auch in der Sprache," *Materialien zu Ernst Blochs Prinzip Hoffnung*, ed. Burghart Schmidt, edition suhrkamp 111 (Frankfurt am Main: Suhrkamp, 1978) 439.

[53] Schmidt, *Kritik*, 13.

[54] See Gert Ueding, ed., "Blochs Ästhetik des Vorscheins," *Ästhetik des Vorscheins*, by Ernst Bloch (Frankfurt am Main: Suhrkamp, 1974). For the same argument, see also Francesca Vidal, *Kunst als Vermittlung von Welterfahrung. Zur Rekonstruktion der Ästhetik von Ernst Bloch* (Würzburg: Königshausen & Neumann, 1994).

present reality itself.[55] Bloch finds *pre-appearance* in every manifestation of great art, be it in architecture, painting, music, dance, theater, film, or literature. For him, all examples of art contain allegories and symbols of the *pre-appearance*, and these allegories and symbols "are all *themselves still fragments, real fragments, through which process streams unclosed and advances dialectically to further fragmentary forms*" (220). He explains this art-fragment connection by contrasting it to religion:

> Art, with its formations which are always individual and concrete, seeks this perfection only in these formations, with the Total as penetratingly viewed Particular; whereas religion, of course, seeks utopian perfection in totality and places the salvation of the individual matter completely in the Totum, in the: 'I make all things new'. Man is supposed to be born again here, society transformed into Civitas Dei, nature transfigured into the celestial. Whereas art remains rounded, when 'classical', it loves the coastal trip around the given, even when it is Gothic, despite all venturing beyond, it has something balanced, homogenized in it. (215)

Because of its special chance to display ideas of *pre-appearance*, Bloch calls art "a labority [sic!] and also a feast of implemented possibilities" (216) or even "the midwife for epiphanies" (216).[56]

The relationship between art and reality is tested in society, or in Blochian words, "the aesthetic pre-appearance is something which is not decided in poetry, but in society" (216). Since Bloch claims that art has the responsibility to encourage people to change their own societies, they need to first envision the final model of a changed society before they can act. Detlef Horster explains that

---

[55] Peter Brenner, "Kunst als Vor-Schein: Blochs Ästhetik und ihre ontologischen Voraussetzungen," *Literarische Utopie-Entwürfe*, ed. Hiltrud Gnüg, edition suhrkamp 2012 (Frankfurt am Main: Suhrkamp, 1982) 40.

[56] Denis Schmidt claims that it is mainly with Bloch that philosophy has turned to art as a model to help analyze human society because philosophy before Bloch had turned rather to mathematical models. See Denis J. Schmidt, "Kunst, Kritik und die Sprache der Philosophie: Zum Beitrag Blochs," *Philosophische Rundschau* 34 (1987): 299-305.

"the intellectual production has to happen before the real production."[57] Art, therefore, is the medium that allows individuals to try out intellectual productions, or, in other words, art is able to invent visionary fragments of changed communities. This implies that art has the ability to experimentally drive *pre-appearance* to an end. Bloch argues:

> Art is fundamentally defined as real pre-appearance, as an immanent-perfect one—in contrast to religious material. This pre-appearance becomes attainable precisely through the fact that art drives its subject-matter to an end, in plots, situations, and characters, and brings it to a stated resolution in suffering, happiness and meaning. (809)

In regard to literature, Bloch sees utopian ideas in many works that literary criticism generally would not label utopian literature. Again, as I already argued above, Bloch calls these works utopian according to *his* interpretation of the utopian, the concrete *utopian surplus*, not according to the literary definition of the utopian genre. In his essay collection *Literature Is Utopia*, Gert Ueding argues that literary criticism should give up its limiting definition altogether, for all literature is utopian already: Whenever literature portrays reality, it shows the deficiencies of particular circumstances, thus implying that a need for a solution and for change exists.[58] Burghart Schmidt supports Ueding's thesis; he, too, calls for an expansion of the term "utopian" in Bloch's sense to discover new interpretations for literary works.[59] Here again, the concept of the fragment is important. Ueding explains that texts that are utopian in the Blochian sense will never provide readers with completely drawn-out political and economic constructions of societies. On the contrary, they will always provide only

---

[57] Detlef Horster, *Bloch zur Einführung* (Hamburg: Junius Verlag, 1987) 52.

[58] Gert Ueding, "Literatur ist Utopie," *Literatur ist Utopie*, ed. Gert Ueding, edition suhrkamp 935 (Frankfurt am Main: Suhrkamp, 1978) 7. For the same argument, see also Burghart Schmidt, "Utopie ist keine Literaturgattung," in Ueding's essay collection, 17-44.

[59] Schmidt, *Kritik*, 8.

fragments of changes,[60] whether they be partly changed societies or changed protagonists.

With respect to the form and content of utopian texts according to Bloch's theory, it is important to differentiate again between abstract and concrete utopias. Ruth Levitas describes concrete utopias as "reach[ing] forward to a real possible future and involv[ing] not merely wishful but will-full thinking."[61] This implies that whereas abstract utopias depict their new dream landscapes without caring whether a realization is possible at all, or caring where the beginnings for their dream landscapes come from, concrete utopias try to connect their images of a different, better world with the tendencies and possibilities that can be found in the criticized reality and then try to set their beginnings into this reality. Bloch describes the connection between the tendencies of reality and the beginnings of changed circumstances as follows: "...as utopia mediated with process, [the concrete utopia] is concerned to deliver the forms and contents which have already developed in the womb of present society" (623). Therefore, development is one of the most important characteristics of the concrete utopia. Bloch also calls the concrete utopia the utopia of process.

Consequently, literature that can be called utopian in Bloch's sense has to depict protagonists who, because of deficiencies in their own circumstances, get the chance to receive glimpses of the *not-yet-become*. These glimpses awaken their *anticipatory consciousness*, which, in turn, enables them to empower themselves. The process of the self-empowerment itself is the protagonists' spiritual journey. As self-empowered individuals, they start to change their circumstances within their communities.

---

[60] For a discussion, see Gert Ueding, "Das Fragment als literarische Form der Utopie," *Etudes Germaniques* 41.3 (1986): 351-362.

[61] Ruth Levitas, "Educated Hope: Ernst Bloch on Abstract and Concrete Utopia," *Utopian Studies* 1 (1990): 15. For another thorough explanation of the differences between concrete and abstract utopias, see also Hanna Gekle, *Wunsch und Wirklichkeit*, 224f.

Looking at literature in general, Bloch considers fairy tales, especially literary fairy tales, among the most important concrete utopian texts. Here he clearly sees the protagonist's *anticipatory consciousness* displayed, which allows the hero to experience *knowing hope*. This *knowing hope*, in turn, causes him or her to change circumstances. Bloch explains his fairytale ideas as follows:

> All fairytale heroes find happiness, but not all are clearly moved towards this happiness beforehand in the dream of it. Only the heroes of the later … literary fairytales or fairytale legends (with authors as different as Hauff, E.T.A. Hoffmann, Keller) are also fairytale figures in psychological terms, namely of a dreamy, utopian nature. Little Muck in Hauff's story: he went out to *seek* his fortune, he precisely pursued his dream of happiness. (357)

However, for Bloch, *the* work of literature that truly embodies concrete utopian thought is Johann Wolfgang von Goethe's *Faust*. Bloch regards the protagonist's search for the ultimate moment as the concrete utopian program itself: Faust's desire to experience a moment he could address with the words "Stay awhile, you are so fair" expresses every single human's dream for a better life. Bloch writes about the protagonist Faust, "He is the venturer beyond the limits par excellence, yet always enriched by his experience when he has ventured beyond it, and finally saved in his striving. He thus represents the highest example of utopian man, his name remains the best, the most instructive" (1012). Faust's quest for himself can be generalized for all concrete utopian literature in the following motto: "…desire is again and again aroused to perceive oneself as the question, the world as the answer, but also the world as the question and oneself as the answer" (1018).

As Fredric Jameson shows, Bloch's interpretation of Faust leads to the concept of the *collective existence* because Faust dreams of "standing on free ground with free people."[62] As I argued earlier, Bloch does not have an individual's egocentric desires and his or her limited wish fulfillment in mind, but

---

[62] Fredric Jameson, *Marxism and Form. Twentieth-Century Dialectical Theories of Literature* (Princeton: Princeton University Press, 1971) 140.

the liberation of the whole human race. By adding the *collective existence*, the people, to the utopian anticipation, Jameson shows that Bloch adds the political vision to utopia. Otherwise, Bloch's theory might simply look like the portrayal of a protagonist's individual journey to him- or herself.[63] Since Bloch is not interested in mere personal psychoanalytical writing, but rather in the changed human society, this insistence on the political vision is necessary. Applied to concrete utopian texts, it means that somewhere in the text the protagonist has to start to act on a higher level than just the personal.

By considering Goethe's *Faust* the quintessential concrete utopian text, Bloch moves the utopian focus from *place* to *idea*: For him and his utopian ideas, the *fieri* is higher than the *esse*. Bloch regards the process, the journey to "free ground" and not the actual place, as important for concrete utopian literature.

Calvin Jones shows that *Faust* incorporates another essential aspect of Bloch's utopian literature, "the open-ended vision." Jones writes:

> Goethe's utopia remains a rich intimation to be reached after infinite striving. ... Goethe's symbol of the mountain represents the attempt to reach it ... This open-ended vision is crucial to Bloch's view of utopia: its form is still to be attempted, rather than something that can already be fully described, even though artistic representations provide a glimpse of the goal. Art is an allegorical pre-appearance.[64]

Therefore, concrete utopian literature will not display a typical happy ending in which every conflict is solved and the perfect society has finally been created. Fredric Jameson points out that Faust's dream to say to the moment "Stay awhile, you are so fair" is never realized, as one would expect in traditional utopian literature. Jameson argues, "Faust never really does live the moment in question; rather he imagines it as we imagine the poem itself, and the conditional in which

---

[63] Jameson, *Marxism and Form*, 140.

[64] Calvin N. Jones, *Negation and Utopia. The German Volksstück from Raimund to Kroetz* (New York: Peter Lang, 1993) 28.

his fatal words are couched stands as a mark of the essentially analogical character of the fable as a whole."[65] *Faust*'s ending supports Bloch's thesis that constant striving toward change and progress is part of the ultimate human essence. A perfect-place happy ending, however, would give the wrong signal to the reader. It would claim that human history might indeed have a final point where striving is no longer necessary.

Taking Goethe's *Faust* as an example and looking at Bloch's ideas in general, it is possible to specify the requirements for a protagonist in Bloch's concrete utopias. As I have shown, one of Bloch's main ideas asks for the actively involved human being who is able to change his or her circumstances because of a vision. Gert Ueding explains that an aesthetic theory according to Bloch will have to start with the individual as the center.[66] An analysis of the text, therefore, would look at the protagonists who suffer from broken personalities but encounter certain circumstances that first help them to gain new, healed personalities, which, in turn, enable them to receive visions of changed places; with these visions they go on and change their communities to the best for everyone. During his or her journey, the protagonist will have to go through three different stages, which Detlef Horster calls incubation, inspiration, and explication.[67] During incubation, the protagonist will only experience deficiencies without knowing any answer or any direction for a solution. During inspiration, the protagonist will start to dream about changes because of his or her vision of a changed society, but he or she will also know that merely dreaming about a better future will not change anything; he or she will have to get actively involved. During explication, the protagonist will eventually discover him- or herself as the producer of larger human history.

---

[65] Jameson, *Marxism and Form*, 142.

[66] Gert Ueding, "Schein und Vorschein in der Kunst: Zur Ästhetik Ernst Blochs," *Materialien zu Ernst Blochs Prinzip Hoffnung*, ed. Burghart Schmidt, edition suhrkamp 111 (Frankfurt am Main: Suhrkamp, 1978) 446.

[67] Horster, *Bloch zur Einführung*, 57.

Watching the protagonists during their journeys through these three stages, readers are supposed to be inspired toward their own, personal agency in their respective societies. Burghart Schmidt explains that terms such as "internalized idea of utopia" become key ideas in Bloch's theory.[68] Since Bloch claims that the subject of history, the working man or woman, has to learn to understand him- or herself as the producer of history in order to cancel out fate in history (695), the main task of a concrete utopia will be to encourage the reader to discover the tendencies and latencies that concern a future process in his or her own present circumstances. As a result, Bloch believes, readers of concrete utopias will live with constant, revolutionarily change-willing attitudes.

---

[68] Schmidt, *Kritik*, 79.

Chapter 2

A Farewell to a Ghost

Toni Morrison's *Beloved*

Toni Morrison's *Beloved* provides a concrete utopian, and therefore political, inspiration for the reader because it contains the hope and the vision Bloch requires from works of art. Here, Denver, one of the protagonists, becomes the Faustian representative who, because of her vision of a changed future, is able to change devastating circumstances first in her own and then in her community's life.

Although Toni Morrison never mentions Bloch or his utopian theory, she probably would agree with his philosophy. Looking at several interviews Morrison has given and at her own theoretical writing, one can claim that Morrison's ideas of literature parallel Bloch's concrete utopian ideas. Bloch believes that in regard to oppression, an individual first has to experience changes in his or her personal circumstances before he or she can transform any larger society. Literature thereby has the political responsibility to provide fictive role models who experience transformations of their personal circumstances that in turn help them work on the larger society's change. By observing the protagonists' struggles, the readers will, it is hoped, receive inspiration from fiction because the text will help them clarify their own positions and recognize options. Likewise, Morrison requires of literature that it provide an inspiration for the reader for his or her own political action in reality. In her essay "Rootedness," for example, she explains her attitude toward the function of literature:

> If anything I do, in the way of writing novels (or whatever I write) isn't about the village or the community or about you, then it is not about anything. I'm not interested in indulging myself in some private, closed exercise of my imagination that fulfills only the obligation of my personal dreams—which is to say yes, the work must be political.... That's a perjorative term in critical circles now: if a work of art has any political influence in it, somehow it's tainted. My feeling is just the opposite: if it has none, it is tainted.[69]

Like Bloch, Morrison understands that the reader's inspiration will happen only if he or she can actively identify with the text. Regarding the writer's responsibility, Justine Tally claims that one can clearly see this idea applied in Morrison's works because Morrison would argue that literature and the work of the writer "is not just important, but crucial; it is not just informative, but formative; it is not just interesting, it profoundly shapes the perception of the world."[70] That Tally's claim holds true can be seen, for example, in an interview with Claudia Tate in which Morrison says about her own work, "My writing expects, demands participatory reading, and that I think is what literature is supposed to do. It's not just about telling a story; it's about involving the reader.... My language has to have holes and spaces so the reader can come into it. He or she can feel something visceral, see something striking."[71] In regard to the political inspiration for the reader, she

---

[69] Toni Morrison, "Rootedness: The Ancestor as Foundation," *Black Women Writers (1950-1980)*, ed. Mari Evans (New York: Anchor Books, 1984) 344-345.

[70] Justine Tally, Introduction: "All necks are on the line," *The Cambridge Companion to Toni Morrison*, ed. Justine Tally (Cambridge: Cambridge University Press, 2007): 1.

[71] Claudia Tate, "Toni Morrison," *Black Women Writers at Work* (Harpenden, England: Oldcastle Books, 1985) 125.

sees her personal obligation in providing this inspiration specifically for her own people, the African American community. In an interview with Thomas LeClair, she states:

> I write what I have recently begun to call village literature, fiction that is really for the village, for the tribe. Peasant literature for *my* people ... I think long and carefully about what my novels ought to do. They should clarify the roles that have become obscured; they ought to identify those things in the past that are useful and those things that are not; and they ought to give nourishment.[72]

In *Beloved*, Morrison clearly displays her commitment to her own ideas of literature that provides nourishment and direction for the African American community. Claudine Raynaud observes that the novel is not only "about disruption, unsettling, derangement, breaking points, it also projects the obverse of this splintering: mediating, metamorphoses ... passages, seamlessness, communing."[73] Because Morrison meets Bloch in this regard, I will discuss *Beloved* as a concrete utopian text.

Bloch's main concern is the "ultimate true identity of man who has come to himself with his world successfully achieved for him."[74] According to him, however, every concrete utopia can deal only with fragments of the *ultimate true human identity* because a universal and general discussion of human problems would be so broad that no individual at all would be able to recognize his or her own problems. If a concrete utopia really intends to inspire an individual toward change, it cannot attempt to find universal answers. Therefore, a concrete utopia

---

[72] Thomas LeClair, "'The Language Must Not Sweat': A Conversation with Toni Morrison," *Toni Morrison. Critical Perspectives Past and Present*, eds. Henry Louis Gates, Jr. and K.A. Appiah (New York: Amistad, 1993) 370.

[73] Claudine Raynaud, "*Beloved* or the Shifting Shapes of Memory," *The Cambridge Companion to Toni Morrison*, ed. Justine Tally (Cambridge: Cambridge University Press, 2007) 56.

[74] Bloch, *Principle*, 313.

will treat only specific problems that are connected to a particular historical period, place, or group.

In regard to *Beloved*, the fragmental search for the *ultimate true identity* deals with a special problem that the late twentieth-century Black community in the United States faces: Morrison sees that her community suffers from more than just continued economic and racist oppression. She recognizes that many African Americans are also held back from leading fulfilled lives because of their negative attitudes toward themselves based on their negative opinions about their own past. Bernard Bell explains the haunting function of *Beloved*:

> On a sociopsychological level, *Beloved* is the story of Sethe Suggs's quest for social freedom and psychological wholeness. Sethe struggles with the haunting memory of her slave past and the retribution of Beloved, the ghost of the infant daughter that she killed in order to save her from the living death of slavery. On a legendary and mythical level, *Beloved* is a ghost story that frames embedded narratives of the impact of slavery, racism, and sexism on the capacity of love, faith, and community of black families, especially of black women, during the Reconstruction period.[75]

While Bernard Bell limits his impact theory of *Beloved* to the Black community of the Reconstruction period, Morrison casts her net much wider, as she would take Bell's statement and apply it to all generations in postslavery times, including her own, current community. With *Beloved*, Morrison intends to make her own people aware of the negative impact of slavery on "the capacity for love, faith, and community" that has created a negative mindset among them. She wants to encourage her people to accept every part of their own history, not only the positive, strong parts but also the negative, painful ones, thus rediscovering self-affirmation and love of their own community.

---

[75] Bernard W. Bell, "*Beloved*: A Womanist Neo-Slave Narrative; or Multivocal Remembrances of Things Past," *Critical Essay on Toni Morrison's Beloved*, ed. Barbara H. Solomon (New York: G.K. Hall, 1998) 168.

To understand Morrison's project, it is first necessary to clarify her thesis about the negative mindset. Several African American theorists have addressed this issue. The philosopher Cornel West, for example, has repeatedly discussed in his writing the negative mindset that can still be found among Black people. In his *Race Matters*, which deals with such problems and needs of the African American community, West writes:

> To talk about the depressing statistics of unemployment, infant mortality, incarcerations, teenage pregnancy, and violent crime is one thing. But to face up to the monumental eclipse of hope, the unprecedented collapse of meaning, the incredible disregard for human (especially black) life and property in much of black America is something else.
>
> The liberal/conservative discussion conceals the most basic issue now facing black America: the nihilistic threat to its very existence. This threat is not simply a matter of relative economic deprivation and political powerlessness—though economic well-being and political clout are requisites for meaningful black progress. It is primarily a question of speaking to the profound sense of psychological depression, personal worthlessness, and social despair so widespread in black America.[76]

Like Morrison, West believes that one method for overcoming this nihilistic threat would be to remember and work through one's own history and tradition. Barbara Christian echoes Morrison's and West's ideas about the Black spiritual crisis when she argues that "if we want to be whole, we must recall the past, those parts that we want to remember, those parts that we want to forget."[77] Together with bell hooks, West reemphasizes this point in *Breaking Bread*. Here, too, he argues that part of the nihilism in the Black community has been caused by its neglect of its past. He repeats his thesis that a sense of personal worthlessness can only be overcome as follows:

---

[76] Cornel West, *Race Matters* (Boston: Beacon Press, 1993) 12-13.

[77] Barbara Christian, "'Somebody Forgot to Tell,' African American Women's Historical Novels," *Wild Women in the Whirlwind*, eds. Joanne M. Braxton and Andree Nicola McLaughlin (New Brunswick: Rutgers University Press, 1990) 341.

> [What is needed is] a critical discovery and a critical revision of one's past, of one's tradition, of one's history, of one's heritage.... it's very clear that Black people must indeed accent the best of our tradition if we are to make it as people ... There are tremendous impediments and obstacles, very difficult circumstances and conditions, but ... that could lead toward our critical understanding of the past and present and our transformation of the present into a better future.[78]

Such a neglect of the past has been possible because, as Sandi Russell explains about postslavery generations, "For those who managed to carry on, life is only made possible by shutting off some parts of themselves."[79] Furthermore, bell hooks explains that the connection between this neglect and postslavery generations is exactly the point *Beloved* serves to address and to correct; she argues:

> The suffering many Black people experience today is linked to the suffering of the past, to "historical memory." Attempts by Black people to understand that suffering, to come to terms with it, are the conditions which enable a work like Toni Morrison's *Beloved* to receive so much attention. To look back, not just to describe slavery but to try and reconstruct a psycho-social history of its impact has only recently been fully understood as a necessary stage in the process of collective Black self-recovery.[80]

In *Beloved,* Morrison addresses the idea of fighting a nihilistic mindset with the acceptance of one's past by telling the story of Sethe, a runaway slave who is not able to live a meaningful life because she is not able to deal with her past. *Beloved*'s Blochian fragmental search for the *true human identity* is connected to Sethe's denial of her past and her nihilistic attitude about the future. Sethe's problem goes back to a murder she committed when her former owner

---

[78] bell hooks and Cornel West, *Breaking Bread. Insurgent Black Intellectual Life* (Boston: South End Press, 1991) 2.

[79] Sandi Russell, *Render Me My Song. African-American Women Writers from Slavery to the Present* (New York: St. Martin's Press, 1990) 112.

[80] hooks and West, *Breaking Bread*, 14.

and three other slave catchers showed up in Ohio after her successful escape from Kentucky. To save her four children from being carried back into slavery, Sethe murdered one of her children, a daughter, and attempted to kill the other three. Some time later, the murdered baby girl comes back as a ghost and haunts Sethe's house.

To understand *Beloved*, one has to read this returned dead daughter as the symbol of the past that comes back one day to haunt the person who has not worked through her past. Brooks Bouson explains that, as Sethe is a victim of trauma, the ghost is Morrison's device "to convey the power of trauma to possess and trap its victims."[81] In Morrison's novel, the dead daughter's spirit first terrorizes Sethe's house for twenty years and then turns herself into a twenty-year old woman named Beloved who shows up at Sethe's door with the intention of slowly but surely ruining Sethe mentally and physically.

I suggested earlier that Denver, Sethe's second daughter who survived the killing, embodies the Faustian representative. For my thesis, it is important to understand that even if *Beloved* is Sethe's story, the Faustian representative is Denver because she serves as the symbol of postslavery generations. Denver does not experience the immediate oppression and exploitation caused by slavery. Rather, Denver's negative circumstances are a product of her immediate community's failure to deal with its slavery past. By presenting Denver as an additional victim of their past, Morrison demonstrates the complexity of the oppression African Americans have had to experience, the immensity of which damages even emerging generations. This idea explains Morrison's purpose of giving *Beloved* to her contemporary African American readership—one of many

---

[81] J. Brooks Bouson, *Quiet as It's Kept. Shame, Trauma and Race in the Novels of Toni Morrison* (New York: State University of New York Press, 2000): 134. For the idea that the ghost should be read as Sethe's trauma, see also the trauma studies by Cathy Caruth, who argues that the "haunting power" of trauma means "precisely to be possessed by an image or event." See Cathy Caruth, Introduction, *Psychoanalysis, Culture and Trauma*, ed. Cathy Caruth, special issue of *American Imago* 48.1 (1991): 3. For an in-depth discussion of Caruth's trauma theory, see also Petar Ramadanovic's "When '*to die in freedom*' Is Written in English: Cathy Caruth's *Unclaimed Experience*," *Forgetting Futures. On Memory, Trauma, and Identity* (Lanham: Lexington Books, 2001): 81-96.

postslavery generations—to help them overcome the still haunting shadows of slavery. Keeping Morrison's purpose in mind, a reading of *Beloved* as a concrete utopia with an intended political inspiration for its recipients is necessarily connected to Denver as the Faustian person.

Bloch demands that the Faustian representative grow into an active character who improves her environment because of her vision of a better future. Denver fulfills this concrete utopian task. She recovers from a passivity toward her community and experiences a transformation from the deliberately chosen existence of a deaf, mute, and passive girl to that of an active woman who has gained self-confidence and independence. She provides Sethe and other community members with the opportunity to recover from the wounds inflicted by an accusing past. She helps her community progressively lose its biases toward Sethe and reunites the Black women in her community. These women had forgotten the idea of support and love for each other, but because of Denver, they exorcise evil, in this case the ghost, from their midst.

To understand the thesis that Denver's life is influenced by the suffering of others, one must first analyze her immediate community's circumstances. Morrison places Denver into an environment in which people are still haunted by their slavery past. In addition to Sethe, several other characters experienced slavery firsthand, including Baby Suggs, Denver's grandmother and Sethe's mother-in-law; Stamp Paid and Ella, both neighbors in Ohio; and Paul D, a fellow slave from the slave farm Sweet Home in Kentucky.

Like Sethe, they have not yet learned to deal with their brutal and depressing past in a way that would allow them to accept their memories and not be paralyzed by them. They have not learned to "lay em down. Sword and shield. Down. Down. Both of em down.... Don't study war no more" (91),[82] as Baby Suggs puts it. All of these former slaves still suffer from the fact that slavery has

---

[82] All references to *Beloved* in this chapter will be given in parentheses in the text and will be cited from the following edition: Toni Morrison, *Beloved* (New York: Plume, 1988).

robbed them of a sense of their own self-worth and self-respect as human beings. Baby Suggs's dream "to love and be loved, to counsel and be counseled, to protect and be protected, feed and be fed" (186) was never an option for them during their bondage. They were not permitted to experience self-determined adulthood, including decisions such as where to live and how to live. White people could violate a Black person's most basic rights any way they wanted to. Sethe explains that "anybody white could take your whole self for anything that came to mind. Not just work, kill, or maim you, but dirty you. Dirty you so bad you couldn't like yourself anymore. Dirty you so bad you forgot who you were and couldn't think it up" (264).

Most of all, however, these former slaves still suffer from the fact that they were denied the concept of living with loved ones as family. In many cases, they were not allowed to choose their partner or when to start and end a relationship because "men and women were moved around like checkers" (24), as Baby Suggs explains. They could not lay claim to their spouses and children because slave holders treated them like cattle. Morrison tells about Baby Suggs, for instance, that "[a]nybody Baby Suggs knew, let alone loved, who hadn't run off or been hanged, got rented out, loaned out, bought up, brought back, stored up, mortgaged, won, stolen, or seized. So Baby's eight children had six fathers" (24). But not only adults were moved around the way a farmer would do with his cattle; Baby Suggs had to witness that "nobody stopped playing checkers just because the pieces included her children" (24). Because of such treatment of their personal relationships, all these former slaves developed, to protect their mental health, a nihilistic attitude toward love of themselves and love of others. Paul D sums it up when he states that for Black people, love is "risky … very risky" (48).

Paul D himself presents an example of the mental agony over lost love that former slaves have to suffer even many years after slavery. Because of his attempt to stay sane, he has developed an attitude that refuses to acknowledge emotions. He believes that "the best thing was to love just a little bit; everything, just a little bit, so when they broke its back, or shoved it in a croaker sack, well, maybe you'd have a little love left over for the next one" (48). As a result of his emotional shutdown, he cannot imagine living "with a woman—any woman—for over two out of three months" (43). At the same time, however, he also suffers from this loss and longs for a place he can call home and for a group he can call family. He recalls that once in Maryland he met "four families of slaves who had all been together for a hundred years, great-grands, grands, mothers, fathers, aunts, uncles, cousins, children.... He watched them with awe and envy, and each time he discovered large families of black people he made them identify over and over who each was, what relation, who, in fact, belonged to whom" (230). About his own family, he can only say, "Mother. Father. Didn't remember the one. Never saw the other. [I] was the youngest of three half-brothers (same mother—different fathers)" (230). Not having any other option, he has become "resigned to life without aunts, cousins, children" (232). When we meet him in *Beloved*, eighteen years after his attempted escape from Sweet Home and now a free man in postslavery time, he is broken in spirit and has resigned himself to a future without visions or hopes. His past has caused him to "shut down a generous portion of his head, operating on the part that helped him walk, eat, sleep, sing. If he could do those things—with a little work and a little sex thrown in—he asked for no more" (43). He deals with his past by locking away all his memories; he has put all his memories "one by one, into the tobacco tin lodged in his chest. By the time he got to 124 [Sethe's residence] nothing in this world could pry it open" (119).

Stamp Paid, another escaped slave, manages his past and his self-hatred by simply declaring his original person as dead. Once his name was Joshua, but he renamed himself when he had to hand over his wife to his master's son. Although Stamp Paid expressed his anger like any other husband, "I should have killed him" (245), he knew that this was not an option for him. Instead, he had to realize that as a slave he did not have the power to defend his or his wife's dignity. When he recognized that his hurt pride and powerlessness caused him to turn his frustration toward his wife, the victim, instead of toward the perpetrator, the master's son—many years later he tells Paul D, "I looked at the back of her neck. She had a real small neck. I decided to break it" (245)—he declared the old Joshua as dead. The new man, Stamp Paid, is not married and does not owe anything to anyone. As a personal revenge on slavery, he escapes north and begins to work for the Underground Railroad. However, he has never again felt able to begin another love relationship.

In addition to the suffering Paul D and Stamp Paid have had to experience, Morrison delineates a particular form of mental brutality that happened to Black women during slavery: The system of slavery completely robbed them of their natural right to self-determined motherhood. They were often forced into pregnancies by brutal rapes. Morrison tells that in many cases the female slaves refused to love the children from these connections. Ella, for instance, was locked up for several years by a strange father/son couple, "the lowest yet" (269). She still remembers that "she had been beaten every way … She remember[s] the bottom teeth she had lost to the brake and the scars from the bell were thick as rope around her waist" (272). The child from this connection, a "hairy white thing, fathered by 'the lowest yet,'" (272) died after five days because Ella refused to nurse it, thereby turning down her forced role as a mother.

Sethe's mother, too, rejected her forced motherhood caused by rape. Sethe knows that her mother bore many babies as a result of innumerable rapes. One of her mother's fellow slaves once told little Sethe about her mother, "She threw them all away but you. The one from the crew she threw away on the island. The others from more whites she also threw away. Without names, she threw them. You she gave the name of the black man. She put her arms around him. The others she did not put her arms around. Never. Never" (66).

In addition to rape and resulting pregnancies, the female slave was regarded as merely a piece of property and consequently reduced to a biological function. Possessing the capacity of reproducing living chattel for her owners, she had to accumulate additional wealth for them. This additional form of psychological exploitation implied that slave mothers were not allowed to claim their children as their own and develop a lasting love relationship with them by living together with their children and watching them grow up. Because Sethe's mother was denied the natural right of an intimate mother-child relationship, Sethe saw her mother only twice in her life: once, when she "was pointed out to her by the eight-year-old child who watched over the young ones—pointed out as the one among many backs turned away from her, stooping in a watery field" (32), and again when Sethe's mother revealed to her the burn mark she bore under her breast, hoping that the sign would become a form of remembrance for her child. She told little Sethe, "This is your ma'am. This ... I am the only one got this mark now. The rest dead. If something happens to me and you can't tell me by my face, you can know me by this mark" (65). But the sign her mother had revealed to her, hoping to establish a memory of an intimidate mother-daughter connection, did not fulfill its designation. When her mother was executed, little Sethe was not able to identity one of the dead bodies as her mother because another slave woman "took her hand and yanked her away from the pile before she could make out the mark" (66).

Like Sethe's mother, Baby Suggs, too, was robbed of her right to self-determined motherhood; she, too, was denied the enjoyment of keeping her children and watching them grow up. Instead, she had to watch all but one of her children being sold away or traded for lumber before they even "had their adult teeth" (24). She tells Sethe, "I had eight. Every one of them gone away from me. Four taken, four chased ... My first-born. All I can remember of her is how she loved the burned bottom of bread" (5/6). Baby Suggs's thoughts about lost motherhood clearly depict the mental agony a slave mother was forced to endure. Even many years after losing her children, Baby Suggs does not reminisce in joy about her motherhood, but only in sorrow:

> The last of her children, whom she barely glanced at when he was born because it wasn't worth the trouble to try to learn features you would never see change into adulthood anyway. Seven times she had done that: held a little foot; examined the fat fingertips with her own—fingers she never saw become the male or female hands a mother would recognize anywhere. She didn't know to this day what their permanent teeth looked like; or how they held their heads when they walked. Did Patty lose her lisp? What color did Famous' skin finally take? Was that a cleft in Jonny's chin or just a dimple that would disappear soon's his jawbone changed? Four girls, and the last time she saw them there was no hair under their arms. Does Ardelia still love the burned bottom of bread? (146)

Sethe, Denver's mother, seems to have been spared the fate of a typical slave mother because she "had the amazing luck of six whole years of marriage to that 'somebody' son who had fathered every one of her children" (25). This was possible because the owners of Sweet Home, the Garners, prided themselves on the idea that their way of slavery was different, simply better and "nicer" than normal slavery.

But the idea of humane, family-oriented slavery acted out at Sweet Home had been an illusion that was destroyed immediately with Mr. Garner's death. Schoolteacher, Mr. Garner's brother-in-law and the new caretaker of Sweet Home, follows the general philosophy of slavery that regards Black people as cattle and treats them accordingly. One of Paul D's brothers, for example, is immediately sold to pay off debts. Concerning Sethe, Schoolteacher thinks of her only as "the breeding one" (238), who still has at least ten fruitful years left—a promising prospect for him. Soon Sethe has to realize that her small happiness of having a real family with four children and a husband cannot hold forever. She understands that with Schoolteacher ruling Sweet Home, her children will have to face the same fate all other slaves have had to experience: They will lose their family and will be stripped of their dignity as human beings. This knowledge causes Sethe's decision to escape from bondage to freedom.

But then, after the arrival of her former "owner" and three other slave catchers at her new home in Cincinnati, Ohio, the same knowledge causes her to kill one of her children and to attempt to murder the other ones. She decides that for the fate of her children it will be better to let them die in freedom rather than be taken back to slavery and to a brutal, inhumane life without love and dignity. Many years later, she explains her action by saying that "[w]hites might dirty *her* all right, but not her best thing, her beautiful, magical best thing—the part of her that was clean" (264).

After the murder, Sethe develops feelings of failure and guilt in regard to her motherly love. She is not able to understand the complete system of slavery that grants slave holders limitless power even beyond geographic borders. Instead, she blames herself alone for the death of her child and believes that her motherly love was not strong enough to protect her children. Sethe's confusion about failed love has stayed with her since the murder and has determined every subsequent detail of her everyday life.

Sethe's pain exemplifies the anguish many ex-slaves in her community suffer as well. Although physically free, they have not been able to cast off the mental chains of slavery. Slavery still haunts them because the desperation about denied or failed love and the pain about separation from loved ones still stay with them. Baby Suggs, for instance, states that freedom doesn't "mean a thing" (24) to her, for it is spent without any of her husbands or her eight children.

Interestingly, Baby Suggs is one of very few ex-slaves who are aware of the reasons for their pain. Consequently, she tries to encourage her fellow citizens toward a new mental beginning in freedom: Every Sunday she preaches her great sermon of love to her fellow community members. She tells them to "cry.... For the living and the dead. Just cry," (93) and to love the only thing left to them, themselves:

> Here in this here place; flesh that weeps, laughs; flesh that dances on bare feet in grass. Love it. Love it hard. Yonder they do not love your flesh.

> They despise it. They don't love your eyes; they'd just as soon pick em out. No more do they love the skin on your back. Yonder they flat it. And O my people they do not love your hands. Those they only use, tie, bind, chop off and leave empty. Love your hands! Love them. ... This is flesh I'm talking about here. Flesh that needs to be loved. Feet that need to rest and to dance, backs that need support; shoulders that need arms, strong arms I'm telling you... (93)

But the pain of the past is so overwhelming that even the strong Baby Suggs is not strong enough to overcome it. Looking back at her life, the old Baby Suggs concludes that it does not make sense to try a new beginning of love and healing, for white people will always have the power to destroy Black people's hopes and dreams. She tells Stamp Paid, "Those white things have taken all I had or dreamed and broke my heartstrings too. There is no bad luck in the world but whitefolks" (94). Therefore, she completely gives in to the idea that "her past had been like her present—intolerable" (4) and turns to a nihilism that causes her personality to wither. The nihilistic Baby Suggs retreats to her bed and, "[s]uspended between the nastiness of life and the meanness of the dead, [cannot] get interested in leaving life or living it" (4).

Like Baby Suggs, many other ex-slaves give in to nihilism, to the "loss of hope and absence of meaning."[83] For example, Paul D is tired of life because it causes too much pain. He wishes that he had died in the lynching fire together with Sixo, his fellow slave at Sweet Home, since "surrender was bound to come anyway, why not meet it with a laugh.... Why the delay?" (230).

Likewise, Sethe considers her free life a burden because her present is dominated by the negative events of her past. Sethe's greatest wish is to forget her past with its mostly negative memories. She attempts to repress those memories by simply not dealing with her past. Her kneading dough for the restaurant's daily menu, for example, serves her as a tool for escape; she perceives it as "nothing better than that to start the day's serious work of beating back the past" (77).

---

[83] West, *Race Matters*, 15.

However, such repression is not possible for her; she tells Denver that her memories always come back to torture her:

> Some things you forget. Other things you never do.... I mean, even if I don't think it, even if I die, the picture of what I did, or knew, or saw is still out there.... The picture is still there and what's more, if you go there and stand in the place where it was, it will happen again; it will be there for you, waiting for you ... even so it is all over—over and done with—it is going to always be there waiting for you. (38)

Her haunting memories lead her finally to such a crazy obsession with her past that she refuses to think at all about any possible future and commits herself solely to her obsession. Morrison writes about the nihilistic Sethe that her brain is "not interested in the future. Loaded with the past and hungry for more, it [leaves] her no room to imagine, let alone plan for, the next day" (74). Having no interest in the future—she considers the future useful only as " a matter of keeping the past at bay" (45)—she lives from day to day without expecting anything that would transform her situation and without forcing herself to challenge her situation.

Recalling Ernst Bloch's analysis of hope for the future, one recognizes that Sethe and the other ex-slaves in her community have given up the basic human capacity of *forward dreaming*. By abandoning this particular form of hope, they have deserted the tool that would enable them to actively challenge their circumstances. With such a passive and nihilistic attitude, they also ruin the future for the following generations such as Denver's because instead of turning their pain into a creative force, their personalities have been withered so much that they only have strength to use their frustration against each other. Instead of uniting against their real enemies, they envy each other their small happiness in freedom. Instead of condemning slavery all together, they compete about who carried the worst burden in slavery. For instance, Morrison tells about their envy of Baby Suggs after she invited the whole community to a feast:

> Now to take two buckets of blackberries and make ten, maybe twelve, pies; to have turkey enough for the whole town pretty near, new peas in September, fresh cream but no cow, ice *and* sugar, batter bread, bread pudding, raised bread, shortbread—it made them mad. Loaves and fishes were His powers—they did not belong to an ex-slave who had probably never carried one hundred pounds to the scale, or picked okra with a baby on her back. Who had never been lashed by a ten-year-old whiteboy as God knows they had. Who had not escaped slavery—had, in fact, been *bought out* of it by a doting son and *driven* to the Ohio River in a wagon ... and rented a house with *two* floors *and* a well.... It made them furious.... Whispered to each other in the yards about fat rats, doom and uncalled-for pride. (144-45)

Yet by blaming each other for their miseries instead of understanding their past, they cause each other additional agony. For example, after the baby's murder, they completely ostracize Sethe and her family.

The community's hate and rejection cause the young Denver to turn into an introverted, nihilistic person, too. Morrison effectively depicts how the connections between Sethe's crime and the community's denouncement cause Denver's personality to shrivel. Because of the community's distancing itself, Denver has to realize that in her home exists "no more lamp all night long, or neighbors dropping by. No low conversation after supper. No watched barefoot children playing in the shoes of strangers" (94). Negative reactions on the community's part, such as "outside a driver whipped his horse into the gallop local people felt necessary when they passed 124" (4), become normal experiences in Denver's life. Even Baby Suggs's funeral is misused for a demonstration of the hostility between Sethe and her community. Denver has to witness the following:

> ...the setting-up was held in the yard because nobody besides [Stamp Paid] would enter 124—an injury Sethe answered with another by refusing to attend the service Reverend Pike presided over. She went instead to the gravesite, whose silence she competed with as she stood there not joining in the hymns the others sang with all their hearts. That insult spawned another by the mourners: back in the yard of 124, they ate the food they

> brought and did not touch Sethe's, who did not touch theirs and forbade Denver to. (179)

Already as a seven-year-old, Denver has to learn that the community does not limit its denouncement to her mother alone but transfers it even to the innocent next generation. The community already blames Denver just for being Sethe's daughter. For example, in Lady Jones's home school, which Denver attends for about a year, she has to realize that she is "being avoided by her classmates—that they made excuses and altered their pace not to walk with her" (108). One of the students, Nelson Lord, asks her the question that will have disastrous consequences for her self-esteem. He wants to know whether her mother indeed killed her baby sister and whether she, Denver, had to stay together with her mother in jail. Unaware of her mother's crime until this point, Denver is tremendously frightened by the idea that this question might contain some unknown truth. Instead of finding out the answer to Nelson Lord's question, she is so scared so much that she prefers to retreat completely to her home and to her inner self than to go back to school. For the next twelve years, she refuses to leave the house at all and turns herself into a deaf and mute person by simply not talking anymore. Contemplating her refusal of the outside world, Denver concludes, "Whatever it is, it comes from outside this house, outside the yard, and it can come right on in the yard if it wants to. So I never leave this house and I watch over the yard, so it can't happen again and my mother won't have to kill me too. Not since Miss Lady Jones' house have I left 124 by myself. Never" (215).

Over the years, Denver learns to understand that the community's attitude is actually a reaction toward her mother and is transferred to her only because she is Sethe's daughter. The following conversation between Sethe and the grown-up Denver reveals Denver's realization:

> -- I can't no more. I can't no more.
> -- Can't what? What can't you?

> -- I can't live here. I don't know where to go or what to do, but I can't live here. Nobody speaks to us. Nobody comes by. Boys don't like me. Girls don't either.... It's the house. People don't—
>
> -- It's not! It's not the house. It's us! And it's you! (15)

In concrete utopian literature that claims to incorporate a political inspiration for the reader, the protagonist has to have a vision of an improved future that causes him or her to change personal and societal conditions. Empowered by this vision, the protagonist who suffers personal oppression will first try to create new, improved circumstances for him- or herself and then go and change his or her community to the best for everyone. In *Beloved*'s specific case, this implies that Denver has to have a vision that allows her to see herself as liberated from her passive, introverted, and nihilistic attitudes. Regarding her community's changes, this vision has to help her accomplish two tasks. First, Denver has to assist her mother to accept her negative past without allowing any guilty feelings to ruin her present. Second, Denver has to influence her fellow citizens to stop their hatred and ostracism of Sethe and instead learn to see Sethe's past as part of their own, thus uniting against their enemy, the white hostile society.

Denver's discovery of her vision is directly related to her dead sister's transformation from a spirit to a personified ghost who shows up one day at Sethe's house. This materialized ghost, who calls herself Beloved—the name inscribed on Sethe's dead daughter's gravestone—serves as a catalyst for Denver and her vision. Margaret Atwood identifies Beloved as the "catalyst for revelations as well as self-revelations."[84] Beloved has come with the intention to take revenge on Sethe by ruining her physically and mentally. Beloved's negative intention will cause Denver to realize that she herself has to be the one who stands up and fights against this evil in her mother's house. Denver's realization of agency is the foundation for Denver's vision.

---

[84] Margaret Atwood, "Haunted by Their Nightmares," Rev. of *Beloved*, by Toni Morrison, *New York Times*, 13 September 1987, 48.

The first act of Denver's agency resulting from Beloved's function as catalyst may be observed on the very first day Beloved arrives. At this point, Denver still assumes that Beloved has come back from the dead because she longs to be reunited with her family, thus also implying a remedy for Denver's loneliness. Therefore, Denver makes it her personal responsibility to care for Beloved, who pretends to be seriously ill. Through this service, Denver develops an alertness that surprises her mother, who has never seen this liveliness in her normally shy and introverted daughter. Here Beloved's function as a catalyst for Denver's development toward self-esteem can be recognized. In caring for the person with whom she has fallen in love, Denver actually starts to care for herself. By fighting against Beloved's disease, she develops a new strength and resistance that has previously been unknown to her. Sethe notices that "Denver tended [Beloved], watched her sound sleep, listened to her labored breathing and, out of love and a breakneck possessiveness that charged her, hid like a personal blemish Beloved's incontinence. She rinsed the sheets secretly.... So intent was her nursing, she forgot to eat or visit the emerald closet" (57). With astonishment, Sethe recognizes that "patience, something Denver had never known, overtook her. As long as her mother did not interfere, she was a model of compassion" (58).

However, only insofar as Denver progressively distances herself from Beloved will she be able to change circumstances for herself and her mother. This distancing indeed happens because, first, Denver has to observe her own exclusion from first Beloved's and then even Sethe's interest; second, Denver begins to recognize Beloved's true intention, the destruction of Sethe. Concerning her exclusion, Denver soon realizes that her interest in a friendship with Beloved is not returned. Step by step, Beloved keeps cutting Denver out of her interest until finally Beloved focuses her attention solely on Sethe. In Beloved's *Song of Songs* for Sethe, "I am Beloved and she is mine" (221), Denver is not mentioned at all. Furthermore, in the games that serve as Sethe's and Beloved's daily occupations, like the "cooking games, the sewing games, the hair and dressing-up games" (251), Denver is excluded not only by Beloved but also by Sethe. Possessed by her sense of guilt, Sethe completely turns to Beloved and, consequently, away from Denver. Daily now, Denver has to experience the following:

> Sethe played all the harder with Beloved, who never got enough of anything: lullabies, new stitches, the bottom of the cake bowl, the top of the milk. If the hen had only two eggs, she got both. It was as though her mother had lost her mind ... she cut Denver out completely. Even the song she used to sing to Denver she sang for Beloved alone. (252)

In addition, Beloved begins to execute her plan of destroying Sethe. Denver observes that Beloved knows exactly where to find Sethe's vulnerable spots because Beloved repeatedly asks Sethe for details about the past; Denver notices "how greedy she [is] to hear Sethe talk" (67). By forcing Sethe more and more into stories of a past that Sethe is desperately trying to forget, Beloved deepens Sethe's pain and her sense of guilt. After some time, Beloved's and Sethe's reciprocal obsession increases to such a point that their relationship turns into a devastating affair. They cause first Paul D to leave and then Sethe's boss to dismiss Sethe from her job at the restaurant. Beloved perfects her torture of Sethe to the degree that Denver fears her mother has gone insane. Morrison tells about Sethe's and Beloved's relationship:

> If the white people of Cincinnati had allowed Negroes into their lunatic asylum they could have found candidates in 124. ...the women had arrived at a doomsday truce designed by the devil. Beloved sat around, ate, went from bed to bed. Sometimes she screamed, "Rain! Rain!" and clawed her throat until rubies of blood opened there, made brighter by her midnight skin. Then Sethe shouted, "No!" and knocked over chairs to get to her and wipe the jewels away. (263)

Every day now, Denver observes that "Sethe no longer combed her hair or splashed her face with water. She sat in the chair licking her lips like a chastised child while Beloved ate up her life, took it, swelled up with it, grew taller on it" (263). Watching the craziness of the two women, Denver perceives that Beloved means neither salvation for her mother nor a remedy against loneliness for herself. Denver finally understands that Beloved intends to kill her mother.

This knowledge provides the final stimulation for Denver's transformation: Fearing to lose the last person who loves her, Denver cannot and will not bear the definite destruction of her mother. Consequently, she decides that she has to take active steps to stop Beloved. Denver comprehends that she has to function as the person who "would have to leave the yard; step off the edge of the world, leave the two behind and go ask somebody for help" (255).

As I mentioned earlier, Denver's problem is her retreat from the outside world. She has experienced too often a community that has displayed hostile attitudes toward Sethe and her family so that "just about everybody in town was longing for Sethe to come on difficult times" (179). Therefore, a transformation of Denver's personality also implies that she has to face the treatment of her hostile community. On her way to asking for help, Denver's first encounter with a neighbor proves that her community is indeed still ostracizing her, even after many years; this neighbor, "standing at the open door, lifted her hand halfway in greeting, then froze it near her shoulder as she leaned forward to see whom she waved to" (257).

However, empowered by her vision of agency, Denver does not allow her first encounter with the outside world to discourage her. Instead, she continues her journey to request help, thus reaching a milestone in her development toward self-esteem, for she has forced herself to leave the house after twelve years. Her journey proves that she is beginning to liberate herself from the anxieties and the inferiority complex that have separated her from society for so long.

Denver's request for help serves also as an initial step for the community's transformation. It not only starts to heal Denver, but it simultaneously helps the community recover from its biases cultivated during the last twenty years, for her neighbors slowly realize the enormous amount of courage it has taken Denver to come and ask *them* for help. They recognize that Denver does not come in arrogance but in humility. Understanding that their neglect of a community member and her family should stop when these people humbly reach out for help, the Black townspeople, as their first step, organize a regular food line for Denver and her family because they are starving. To show her thankfulness and her appreciation of the community's support, Denver visits every single person who has supplied something. Her approach to every individual person carries forward the transformation process and serves two purposes: It continues Denver's own development, for she is steadily losing her shyness and awkwardness she previously displayed when encountering the outside world, and it helps the people in her community gradually overcome their biases. Morrison writes about the neighbors, "They whispered, naturally, wondered, shook their heads. Some even laughed outright at Denver's clothes of a hussy, but it didn't stop them caring whether she ate and it didn't stop the pleasure they took in her soft 'Thank you'" (262).

Denver's personal transformation reaches its climax when she decides that she should no longer depend on her community's kindness but should instead find employment to support herself and her family. Her decision demonstrates that she has indeed gained the self-reliance and independence necessary for a mature personality. Denver's encounter with Paul D after her transformation proves that she is able to pass the test for her newly gained personality. Formerly knowing her as rather cold toward him and other people, Paul D now observes that "she was the first to smile. 'Good morning, Mr. D.' … Her smile, no longer the sneer he remembered had welcome in it" (280). As an additional example, Morrison uses Stamp Paid to testify to Denver's new identity. Stamp Paid, who has known Denver since the day she was born, for he shipped Sethe over the Ohio River toward freedom, concludes about Denver and her new self, "I'm proud of her. She turning out fine. Fine" (280).

However, to provide the reader with the political inspiration Bloch asks for, *Beloved* has to show that Denver's transformation challenges others toward their own personal transformation and toward the idea that they themselves originate more changes. Denver succeeds in this regard, too. Ella, for instance, represents such an example of a fellow citizen who is transformed by Denver and who in turn initiates more changes. Ella, Sethe's once-upon-a-time friend, had turned completely against Sethe after the baby's murder because, as Bernhard Bell argues about her, Ella might believe "in root medicine but not love."[85] After Sethe got out of jail, Ella "junked her and wouldn't give her the time of day" (269). But now, twenty years later, Ella watches Denver and reasons that "the daughter, however, appeared to have some sense after all. At least she had stepped out of the door, asked for the help she needed and wanted work" (269). Paying close attention to Denver's domestic circumstances, Ella realizes that Denver alone is unable to help Sethe free herself from Beloved, the symbol for Sethe's accusing past. Therefore, Ella gives up her twenty-year-old rejection of Sethe and convinces the other Black women that "rescue [is] in order" (269).

The exorcism of the ghost presents another highlight in the community's transformation. To rightfully call Sethe's community a transformed community, it is not enough for the townspeople to merely supply food but otherwise watch Sethe's mental destruction by Beloved. On the contrary, the existence of Beloved in Sethe's house challenges the community at large about their true transformation because, as Naomi Rand explains, "They must admit that [Beloved] is a part of everyone's history, a living embodiment of their past. Thus Beloved's appearance makes demands on Sethe and all those around her."[86]

---

[85] Bell, "*Beloved*: A Womanist Neo-Slave Narrative," 172.

[86] Naomi Rand, "Surviving What Haunts You: The Art of Invisibility in *Ceremony*, *The Ghost Writer* and *Beloved*," *MELUS* 20.3 (Fall 1995): 24.

Realizing their "shared suffering and finally the sense of community,"[87] thirty women combine their power and succeed in exorcising the ghost. By doing so, they demonstrate that they have learned to rely on each other and work together. Betty Jane Powell maintains that this "gathering together of individual voices into a coherent unit expels the past at least to a point that will allow healing."[88]

Since Sethe's and Denver's community members have rediscovered the idea of sisterhood and have experienced the realistic chance of self-empowerment, healing is now possible among them with each other. In addition, there is indeed realistic hope that they will continue to live out the idea of supporting community for other future challenges.

Denver's transformation also helps Paul D find hope for a meaningful future for himself. Like Sethe, he is unable to imagine a future that is worth living for because he is too busy suffering from a past he cannot accept. After a failed escape from the slave farm Sweet Home in Kentucky, he had to watch the murders of his brothers Paul F and his friend Sixo and see Halle, Sethe's husband, turn crazy. After spending ten years in a horrible jail in Georgia, from which he was able to escape, and fleeing for eight years from one place to another, he begins to believe that his past presents one of the worst experiences a Black person has been forced to have. Consequently, he develops a nihilistic outlook on his future.

At first, it seems that moving in with Sethe has helped him give up this destructive attitude and find hope necessary for a new start because when he arrives at Sethe's house and listens to her thoughts about the jumbled order of past and present, he offers her a new beginning for the future. He tells her, "Sethe, if

---

[87] Rand, "Surviving What Haunts You," 30.

[88] Betty Jane Powell, "'Will the parts hold?': The Journey toward a Coherent Self in *Beloved*," *Understanding Toni Morrison's Beloved and Sula*, eds. Solomon O. Iyasere and Marla W. Iyasere (Troy, NY: Whitston Publishing Company, 2000) 152.

I'm here with you, with Denver, you can go anywhere you want. Jump, if you want to, 'cause I'll catch you, girl. I'll catch you 'fore you fall: Go as far inside as you need to, I'll hold your ankles ... we can make a life. A life" (49). But when he learns the details about Sethe's story of the baby's murder, he is so shocked that he reacts like everybody else and simply condemns her. He decides that a future with someone like Sethe is not worthwhile and consequently separates from her. After his departure, he turns himself over to a form of nihilism that is even worse than the one he had lived with before he arrived at Sethe's house. Stamp Paid finds him one day living in a basement with alcohol as his sole companion now.

However, because of a changed Denver and a transformed community, Paul D is inspired to rethink his attitudes toward Sethe, his own past, and his inability to imagine a meaningful future for himself. He begins to understand that accepting the past is possible. Because of Denver, he discovers that "just beyond his knowing is the glare of an outside thing that embraces while it accuses" (285). This outside thing is *his* past, which tells him that he has wronged Sethe by reacting with the same misunderstanding and denouncement that Sethe's community has displayed toward her without even listening to her point of view. But this past also embraces him: It offers him healing from its evil memories. Hence, he does not need to run away from his memories any longer but can accept the negative events as belonging to a time that lies behind him, thereby clearing his mind for a time that lies before him. When Paul D tells Sethe, "...me and you, we got more yesterday than anybody. We need some kind of tomorrow," (288) he demonstrates that he is able to put the past into the correct place and is now able to imagine a challenging and fulfilling future for them to share.

Paul D's second offer to Sethe about a shared tomorrow points to the fact that Sethe still needs a lot of help from others to give up her nihilism. When Paul D returns to her, she is only able to reply, "I'm tired, Paul D. So tired. I have to rest a while.... Oh, I don't have no plans. No plans at all" (286). Unlike Denver and Paul D, Sethe has not yet been able to transform her life and find peace for her suffering soul. Morrison ends her novel with the following:

> By and by all trace is gone, and what is forgotten is not only the footprints but the water too and what it is down there. The rest is weather. Not the breath of the disremembered and unaccounted for, but wind in the eaves, or spring ice thawing too quickly. Just weather. Certainly no clamor for a kiss.
>
> Beloved. (290)

One could assume that Morrison's ending does not allow the reader to hope for Sethe's healing, or even worse, does not allow hope for the continuation of the community's road toward transformation, toward the future of the *not-yet-*become. Morrison's ending seems to point too much toward forgetting, a thing the community was supposed to overcome. However, in his study about the connection between trauma and *Beloved*, Petar Ramadanovic points out that Morrison's ending does in fact imply the hope for a sustainable transformation. He argues:

> Beloved's return cannot replace properly that which was replaced, nor can it recuperate or gather that which was fragmented, nor, which amounts to the same thing, can it represent the past. What her or its appearance can do is to recall this community of ex-slaves to the past. What Beloved does, in other words, is to actualize a long-gone event, perform its remembering and forgetting, and thus come to the verge of representing it.[89]

Therefore, Morrison's ending is not about forgetting to put the past into the correct perspective, but about letting the catalyst go. There is hope that Sethe will recover from her past wounds. Because of Denver, Paul D, and her community, at some point in the future, Sethe might indeed accept her painful past and her memories.

---

[89] Petar Ramadanovic, "In the Future: Reading for Trauma in Toni Morrison's *Beloved*," *Forgetting Futures. On Memory, Trauma, and Identity* (Lanham: Lexington Books, 2001) 103.

During her own life, Baby Suggs could see only for a very short time her dream "to belong to a community of other free Negroes—to love and be loved by them, to counsel and be counseled, to protect and be protected, feed and be fed" (186) become reality. Her dream had the potential to become the Faustian dream, "to stand on free ground with free people," which offers, according to Bloch, the dream of the *ultimate true human identity*. Yet Baby Suggs soon had to realize that her own community destroyed the idea. However, because of Denver's vision and agency, Baby Suggs's dream finally becomes the chance to serve as inspiration of Blochian glimpses of the *not-yet-become* for Denver, Sethe, Paul D, and their fellow citizens. This new community has not turned into a perfect society and never will, but their rediscovered sense of mutual support provides them with Blochian glimpses of the *not-yet-become*. These glimpses, together with the resulting capability of *forward dreaming*, will help *Beloved*'s Black townspeople face future challenges.

Chapter 3

The Creation of a Messiah

Gloria Naylor's *Bailey's Café*

In my thesis, I claim that Bloch's concrete utopian idea can be applied to most works by contemporary African American women writers. Yet at first sight, Gloria Naylor's *Bailey's Café*, on the one hand, and Alice Walker's *The Color Purple* and Toni Morrison's *Beloved*, on the other hand, do not seem to offer any similarities that allow one to establish a common theory of African American hope. When comparing Naylor's text with Walker's and Morrison's, one immediately recognizes obvious differences. For their novels, Walker and Morrison chose very specific African American topics: the situation of poor Black women in the South and the mindset of the contemporary Black community with its problematic (non)acceptance of the slavery past, respectively. Both novels mainly depict realistic backgrounds, even if they opt to bring in some non-realistic elements such as Walker's idea of reinstating Celie's dead sister and her family who all drowned while on their way back from Africa to America and Morrison's device of turning the murdered baby girl into a ghost. Naylor, however, takes a different approach. Although most of her characters in *Bailey's*

Café are Black except for Gabe, a Russian Jew, she does not primarily deal with a particular African American topic. Instead, she chooses a surrealistic topic and deals with the dark side of the human soul in general. In *Bailey's Café*, she is foremost interested in the despair and the hopelessness, the broken and deferred dreams humans in general have to experience. Instead of depicting a realistic world, she leads her reader into a completely surrealistic street that can exist anywhere on Earth and can be entered from any point; people walk in "here from the streets of Chicago the same way they walk in from Detroit, Saint Paul, Memphis, or New York" (192)[90] and even from as far away as Addis Ababa in Ethiopia or the Caucasus Mountains in Russia. This strange street consists of only three buildings: Bailey's café, which "sits right on the margin between the edge of the world and infinite possibilities" (113) and has a back door that "opens out to a void" (113); Gabe's pawnshop, which never opens; and Eve's boardinghouse-bordello, which can be joined as a resident only "when you see the garden—if you see the garden" (119).

Nevertheless, although Naylor uses such a radically different, surrealistic approach, I claim that her novel, too, fits into my theory of concrete African American hope in the Blochian sense. By choosing to include *Bailey's Café* in my analysis, I intend to show that novels as diverse as Walker's *The Color Purple* and Morrison's *Beloved*, on the one hand, and Naylor's *Bailey's Café*, on the other hand, do indeed suit my theory. Since Bloch argues that the *utopian surplus*, the hope-content of the human race which transcends all times and events, is not a legacy of a fixed tradition but can actually be found in works of art as different as the Strasbourg Cathedral, the Divine Comedy, or Bach's Mass in B minor, it is clear that novels as different as Walker's, Morrison's, and Naylor's can contain the *utopian surplus*, thereby all providing political inspiration for the reader.

---

[90] All references to *Bailey's Café* in this chapter will be given in parentheses in the text and will be cited from the following edition: Gloria Naylor, *Bailey's Café* (Thorndike, Maine: G.K. Hall & Co., 1992).

In *Bailey's Café*, one can observe Bloch's *principle of hope* at its best. As I mentioned earlier, Bloch claims that society improves only because of individuals who have a vision of changed circumstances and the capacity of *forward dreaming*, thus becoming actively involved in transforming conditions. In *Bailey's Café*, people from the most hopeless circumstances from all over the world enter Naylor's street and have two choices: either they "head to the back of the café and end it" (316) or they "eventually go back out and resume [their] life—hopefully better off when [they] found us" (316). However, such a strengthened return to normal life happens only to people who receive a vision during their visit to Naylor's street, thus echoing Bloch's point about the necessity of a vision as an enabling power for change.[91]

In her book, Naylor tells the stories of several individuals who undertake a spiritual journey from complete despair and hopelessness to optimism for their future. When they enter Bailey's café for the first time, their life stories differ, yet they all share the feeling of hopelessness about personal circumstances. In her review, Karen Joy Fowler states, "A person finds Bailey's when he or, more often, she reaches a certain level of hopelessness."[92] Bailey himself says about his café that someone needs "the blues to get there" (7). During their spiritual journeys, hope helps them to find a vision for their future, thus providing them with the chance to heal from past wounds and to gain enough strength to face old circumstances. Since Naylor's concept matches Bloch's theory of hope in this

[91] That such a reading of Naylor's text through the lenses of Bloch's theory enriches the text can be seen when one compares my application with another analysis. In his reading of *Bailey's Café*, Philip Page acknowledges the initial tremendous misery and the subsequent transformation of the characters discussed here, yet he mainly gives only a description of the different miseries, and his only explanation for their transformation is that these characters learn to accept the abyss, to accept that life offers both sides, good and evil. See Philip Page, "Living with the Abyss in Gloria Naylor's *Bailey's Café*," CLA Journal 40.1 (1996): 21-45.

[92] Karen Joy Fowler, Rev. of *Baileys Café*, by Gloria Naylor, *Gloria Naylor. Critical Perspectives Past and Present*, eds. Henry Louis Gates, Jr. and K.A. Appiah (New York: Amistad, 1993) 26.

point,[93] it is possible to call her characters Faustian representatives who finally reach the Blochian goal of the "true identity of man who has come to himself with his world successfully achieved for him."[94]

For my analysis of *Bailey's Café*, I have chosen several such Faustian representatives. I will discuss the spiritual journeys of five characters: Sadie, a sixty-year-old alcoholic and twenty-five-cent prostitute, whose biggest dream throughout her entire life has been that someone would love her; Esther, who lived in a dark basement for twelve years where she had to perform sadomasochistic acts, which not only caused her to hate all men but also made her unable to live with any form of light; Peaches, who was so overprotected by her jealous father that she developed a strong self-hatred that led later to nymphomania and self-mutilation; Jesse Bell, who married into Black high society but could not deal with its hypocrisy and as a result became a heroin addict; and Miss Maple, a Black male with a Ph.D. in statistics from Stanford, who turned to wearing women's attire after realizing that the business executive world was closed to him.

Faustian representatives, according to Bloch, will transcend the *utopian surplus* to the reader. Yet, looking at the five Faustian characters I have chosen, one might argue that they are too removed from most readers' circumstances to allow such transcendence. However, Charles Wilson argues that although these five characters "may be called misfits when perceived from an assumed position of normalcy, within the confines of the work, each is as normal as his or her circumstances allow. In short, Naylor forces the reader to (re-)consider these

---

[93] Gloria Naylor has often been asked in personal interviews about her strong sense of vision in her writing. Asked by Virginia Fowler, for example, whether she would consider herself something like a biblical prophet, she defined her role "more as a filter." See Virginia Fowler, "A Conversation with Gloria Naylor," *Conversations with Gloria Naylor*, ed. Maxine Lavon Montgomery (Jackson: University Press of Mississippi, 2004) 123. The idea to call herself or her texts "filters" connects her to Bloch; it implies that she allows glimpses of the *not-yet-become* to shine through her writing.

[94] Bloch, *Principle*, 313.

characters in the context of their individual lives."[95] And William Nash even sees such a Blochian-like inspiration for the reader in *Bailey's Café*; he argues that Naylor's text "suggests the possibility for some growth that might lead to real changes in social and cultural definitions of African American identity from both inside and outside the community."[96]

When listening to the protagonists' five stories, the reader is able to recognize Naylor's main thesis: Although Naylor holds American white society partially responsible for the miseries of her protagonists, she also claims that a lot of human misery is caused by ordinary people in the protagonists' immediate surroundings, in many cases by so-called loved ones such as family members or relatives. With *Bailey's Café*, Naylor intends to illustrate that every single human being, even the most ordinary and innocent one, has the capacity to ruin another person's life. According to this premise, she states that she herself would be capable at any moment "right now of the most degrading, the most heinous acts that have ever been perpetrated on this earth. I, Gloria Naylor, am capable of doing what Hitler did, of doing what Idi Amin did."[97] Yet simultaneously, every human being carries also the capacity of choice; while she could choose to be like Hitler, she would also be capable of doing "what Mother Theresa has done, and what Martin Luther King has done."[98] For her novel, she takes this thesis about the human capability of choice and applies it mostly to specific situations in Black people's lives.

---

[95] Charles E. Wilson, *Gloria Naylor. A Critical Companion* (Westport, CT: Greenwood Press, 2001) 127.

[96] William R. Nash, "The Dream Defined: *Bailey's Café* and the Reconstruction of American Cultural Identities," *The Critical Response to Gloria Naylor,* eds. Sharon Felton and Michelle C. Loris (Westport, CT: Greenwood, 1997) 212.

[97] Fowler, "A Conversation with Gloria Naylor," 128.

[98] Fowler, "A Conversation with Gloria Naylor," 128.

As I mentioned earlier, Naylor situates her street in a surrealistic world. For a Blochian concrete utopian reading of *Bailey's Café*, it is important to understand that even if the novel is situated in a street so surrealistic that the reader has the impression that Naylor wants one to focus on the place, the author is foremost interested in spiritual development and considers the street only a "way station" (227). Its buildings represent only necessary tools for the spiritual passages the Faustian representatives have to go through, for they are all people of reality who need the surrealistic street only as a transitional space. Therefore, before analyzing the individual spiritual journeys, one should take a closer look at the street and the peculiar ways it functions to understand how such buildings can guide a Faustian representative during his or her journey.

The café, the boardinghouse-bordello, and the pawnshop all follow some strange rules that one normally would not expect of such places in reality. Gabe's pawnshop, for instance, displays a cardboard sign on its door that "has a painted clock with movable hands [and] reads, Back at __, and each hour [Gabe] keeps moving the hands one hour forward" (207). If a customer still does not get the message and comes back after an hour to buy something, Gabe gets mad at the person. The street even gets stranger with its boardinghouse-bordello, which has the ability to grow in seconds all the flowers its residents wish to see, even if that means summer flowers in winter and vice versa. However, only people with the capacity for dreaming can see the house and its mystical garden.

The café, too, should not be confused with a normal restaurant. The owner, Bailey, deliberately serves bad coffee and bad food so customers will not think they visit this place for the food and the coffee. Moreover, ordering a dish does not imply that a customer gets served; Nadine, Bailey's wife, only serves people "when the mood hits her" (12), and it is hard for customers to figure out when she "is ringing up the register and it's iffy when and how much she'll charge" (12). And some days the building is even gone altogether. Bailey explains the whole philosophy of his café:

> ...folks shouldn't get the wrong idea about this place. If we start serving 'em too readily, they'll begin thinking we're actually in the business of running a café. Forgetting how it happened they stumbled in here, they'll start looking for us when they're hungry. And then when they don't find us, they'll start asking questions. Hey, why wasn't this place here last month when I came by? I could see if you'd just closed down—but the whole damn building was gone. Life's too short to spend time trying to explain the obvious to the idiot. If they can't figure out that we're only here when they need us, they don't need to figure it out. (47)

Indeed, the people who visit Bailey's café do not need the café for its food, but for contemplation: Because the café sits at the end of the world, for many visitors it becomes the last place they can go to rest a while and to rethink options for themselves. The café's back door and its void play a key role in their contemplation processes because entering the void allows those visitors to relive deferred dreams and memories. Their memories are as diverse as the visitors themselves. Sometimes one can hear examples of the most beautiful music from all cultures, such as a "chorus of Christmas carols. The blowing of a shofar. Ghanta bells. Jade gongs. Gong chimes. Or the silver sounds of Tunisian finger cymbals" (232). Sometimes one can observe "small parties or huge parties going on. Sometimes there is mellow candlelight spread over dining-room tables or crystal chandeliers sparkling down on dancing crowds of people with children running among their feet. There is not always a Christmas tree, but there is always laughter" (232).

Reliving broken dreams in the void can have different effects on the visitors. For example, the search for lost memories and old dreams simply overwhelms some of them to such an extent that they decide not to enter reality again and instead commit suicide by staying in the void forever. Bailey tells about this particular group of visitors:

> I can tell if it's gonna be a suicide when the whole thing starts to glow so brightly it hurts your eyes, and the beautiful music gets so dim it hurts your head to strain to hear it.... I know what that particular customer has

> planned: they're going to stay out back until a certain memory becomes just too much to bear. (232)

Gabe, for instance, never enters the void because of this possible danger; he states that "a proper Sabbath meal means family, and that would mean calling up ghosts; and it'd be too tempting just to stay back there forever" (207).

Yet, since the café "sits right on the margin between the edge of the world and infinite possibility" (113), for others the void becomes the place where they have the chance to receive a vision for their future because of certain images they can see in the void. The hopeful visions enable them to gain the necessary strength and courage to go back to their respective lives in reality.

These particular people are the Faustian representatives in *Bailey's Café,* for they execute in their lives the Blochian idea of *men en route* who will eventually *walk upright* because of their experiences in the void. For instance, Jesse Bell's life gets turned around because of her vision in the void: After seeing herself one more time at the beginning of her life as an innocent young girl with many high hopes for her future, Jesse Bell is able at last to give up her heroin addiction. And Miss Maple, who grew up with his grandmother's belief that one is able to see snow in the desert if one truly believes in this vision, eventually sees snow in the desert—in the void. Likewise, Sadie leaves the void as another person because, after dreaming her whole life about a person who would love her, she finally gets her first kiss there.

Like Bailey's café and its void, Eve's boardinghouse-bordello represents a Blochian way station and is thus a necessary tool for the Faustian representative *en route*. However, whereas every desperate person in the world is allowed to enter Bailey's café, Eve's place follows a different philosophy. Whereas Bailey's café gives access even to people who either do not want to continue their lives and instead choose to end them or who just need a break without seriously considering any changes in their circumstances, Eve admits only women who seriously want to improve their personal conditions. The reader learns about Eve's admittance philosophy that “charity has nothing to do with it. Eve is not a charitable person” (118). Instead of accepting every needy woman who is looking for her house, she grants entrance only to women who are able to imagine a different future for themselves, women to whom she can say, “When you see the garden—if you see the garden—you’re there” (119).

Eve’s philosophy matches Bloch’s ideas about the *enabling day dream* that leads one to self-empowerment, which in turn will cause one to work on societal changes. Like Bloch, Eve knows that offering support to people who have not experienced any form of a vision will be in vain. For her, people have “to know about delta dust” (119), which is Eve’s synonym for vision. Otherwise, “there is no need to waste directions on someone who’s just going to spend her life staying lost” (192).

As a result of her philosophy, Eve also turns down women who desperately need a place to stay. For example, Eve reports about a particular woman who showed up at her place with “Lucky Strike spelled out on the inside of her thigh with a lit cigarette butt. A reminder to get the right brand the next time she was sent to the store” (119). This woman told Eve that she had left the brutal Lucky Strike guy for another man “who’d gotten her pregnant before going back to his wife” (119). Nevertheless, Eve turned her down because the woman was not able to imagine a different future for herself where she would walk upright. Eve knew that the woman would never have a vision because “with all that this woman had been through and would still keep going through—they always manage to keep going through it—she didn’t know, just didn’t know, about delta dust” (120). Consequently, only those women who have the capacity to envision a different future, thus empowering themselves, are admitted into Eve’s boardinghouse-bordello.

However, it is not only Eve’s admittance ideas that differ from the ones of a typical bordello in reality. As Bailey has done for his café, Eve has set some strange rules for her house. Nevertheless, her strange rules make perfect sense in regard to the Blochian idea of self-empowerment. Eve's basic idea is to help her women develop strong egos because all the women in her house were mistreated or misused by men. Such treatment was possible because of the women's low self-esteem and lack of self-respect. Consequently, Eve wants her women to develop strong egos and exercise their self-esteem while in her house, thus helping them become able to stand up and ask for respect from all the men they will encounter later when they go back to reality. Therefore, all rules serve the purpose of ego creation.

One of her rules, for example, deals with the customer's fee: Eve insists that every "gentleman caller" has to pay his woman with a fresh bouquet of her favorite flowers because "if he can't do that much for you, he doesn't need to waste your time" (135). Another ego-creating rule concerns the basic acceptance of customers; even though her house is a bordello, Eve does not make her women receive customers. The decision is left entirely to every woman staying there. While Peaches, for instance, sees so many men during one day that they "sit knee to knee in the parlor" (163), Jesse Bell refuses to see any at all: "The men who try to visit her get their flowers smashed right in their faces at the door" (168).

Into this strange street, Naylor places her Faustian representatives. All of them have entered the street because they have experienced unbearable pain inflicted on them by other people. Even the three proprietors of the street, Bailey, Eve, and Gabe, know from personal experience about unbearable pain and despair. Naylor uses them to establish her thesis about the human race before she proves her point with the stories of her other characters. Again Naylor claims that every single human suffering is caused and executed not by some external circumstances or some anonymous constellation, but by normal and ordinary fellow humans.

Gabe, for instance, who survived the Jewish Holocaust but lost his entire family, understands exactly the dark side of human nature that is able to deliberately hurt or ruin another person. When people try to convince him that the Holocaust could have happened only because Hitler was a real monster, Gabe tells them, "No, we are talking about a human being … he was no more than a man. And Hitler had help … life is much too complicated to start pointing fingers; we wouldn't have enough of them" (314).

Gabe's statement leads to Naylor's idea that one does not have to be powerful to cause human suffering. On the contrary, every individual has the capacity to cause enough pain to destroy someone else. Bailey himself serves as an example of this. Since his service in World War II and his participation in the destruction of Hiroshima and Nagasaki, he has known that any argument such as "I'm a soldier. I follow orders" (42) is merely a lie and that one is completely responsible for every single action one undertakes at any point in life. While still in Japan, Bailey tried at first to ignore this fact about personal guilt by attempting to repress his memories of killing people:

> I chewed up the palm of my hand and spat out the blood to keep from dozing at night. I could stop myself from sleeping, so there would be no dreams. But I had to breathe…. I packed dirt up my nose and panted through my mouth. But I could still hear it. The divine wind. Kamikaze. I jammed empty shell casings into my ear canals…. I rolled in the mud, howling up into the hills of Okinawa. Begging for any god to take it all away. (43)

Yet in the end, his attempts were in vain. When the reader meets him in his café many years after Japan, he is still tortured by his memories, which are constantly returning as nightmares—even in the middle of the day when he is not asleep.

Bailey's character even stands for every human being in general because, as one learns in the novel, "Bailey" is not his name. When the man who now calls himself Bailey assumed ownership of the café, he saw that the name was already sketched on the outside of the café, and he decided to adopt it. But the reader never learns his real name. Charles Wilson points to the importance of this fact because "in another context, [Bailey] might be called by another name … the symbol is less important than the signified."[99] Thus, Bailey resumes the role of "everyman" for the observing reader.

Whereas Bailey is guilty himself of destroying others, Eve serves as an example of someone who was destroyed by so-called normal and ordinary people. At one time, Eve experienced a happy childhood full of love and affection from a minister who had found her as an abandoned baby in a patch of ragweed, still tied to the placenta. But her happy and innocent relationship with her stepfather changed when her body began to develop and the women in her town started to ask evil, gossipy questions such as, "Why was he still cooking and cleaning for [her]? Why had he never married? Why was no boy ever allowed to come and call? Or even walk [her] home from church?" (122). As a result of these questions, Eve realized that her stepfather "stop[ped] bathing me on Saturday nights in that old tin tub, and the dark brown homespun he used for making all my dresses was cut loose and fell from the shoulders to the hips. They now hang on me like the ugly brown sacks they were" (122). The end of the Saturday night baths had an especially destroying effect on Eve's emotional life, for they had represented the only occasions when she could come close to some form of the affection a child has a right to receive from her father. From that point, her body and especially her longing soul were deprived of any form of living touch. When her stepfather found Eve and a neighborhood boy engaged in partly still innocent, partly already erotic play in the backyard, he threw her out of his house and his life. Eve comments on his punishment:

> He said I was going to leave him the way he'd found me, naked and hungry.... The first chores I ever did around that house were to haul the wood and build the yard fire where he burned every one of those brown sack dresses he'd sewn for me. And then he made me strip off the one I was wearing—and he burned that, too, along with the cotton underpants and cotton warps I used to bind down my breasts. Those underpants would have been ruined anyway, because then he purged me with jars of warm

---

[99] Wilson, *Gloria Naylor*, 135.

> water and Epsom salts. To remove, he said, every ounce of food his hard work had put into my stomach. (129)

Many years later, Eve understands that in addition to blaming "those righteous, righteous women" (124) in her community for stealing her innocent father-daughter relationship from her, she has to hold her stepfather responsible, too, for destroying her. Even if the neighborhood women are to be partly blamed, he was still solely responsible for every action connected to Eve's forced departure into an unknown world. When throwing her out of his house, the man was fully aware that his action could have meant death for Eve, but he still deliberately sent her away naked into a dangerous future. Like Bailey, he represents an example of an ordinary person—one who would even be considered a good person by normal standards, the local preacher who took in an orphan—who ruins another person's life.

The other protagonists in *Bailey's Café* have also been prevented, because of other, ordinary people, from experiencing fulfilled and meaningful lives full of love and respect. By narrating their stories, Naylor elaborates on her thesis about the human race and its potential for causing suffering.

For example, Sadie, who enters Bailey's café from the south side of Chicago, has been pushed around and rejected all her life by the people from whom she hoped to receive love. Her whole miserable life is a product of denied love and care. As a small girl she has to learn that her mother considers her a burden since Sadie is the result of a failed abortion; consequently, her mother calls her only "The One The Coat Hanger Missed" (64). Sadie's early childhood years are shaped by the experience of this name:

> Not that the woman ever spoke to her, or hardly ever looked at her unless she was drinking—and then only to curse her for the daddy's face she wore. But she'd hear it when one of the men her mother brought home for the night would ask about the sleepy child. She'd hear it when yet another streetwalker would pat her cheek as they moved around that circuit from boardinghouse to boardinghouse, when she spilled her milk, when she

> forgot to tiptoe in the morning, and when she stroked the hair of the drunken woman sprawled over the dirty dishes on the table; she'd hear it after she was slapped and shoved away. The One The Coat Hanger Missed. (64)

When she is old enough to compare her own domestic situation with those of other children, she realizes that other children are not beaten as much as she is and then only when they "weren't good" (66). Therefore, Sadie concludes that it has to be her own fault that her mother does not love her, for she is not a good child. As a result of her conclusion, she decides to become a perfect daughter, hoping that it will cause her mother to love her:

> Now her mama could drag in from the streets and drink herself into a stupor across a clean table; the dishes were all washed and put away. And she always found the sheets on her bed freshly changed if she dragged in a man or not. The child discovered ways to make absolutely no noise. Sadie became so good at being quiet in the morning the woman would have to clear her bleary eyes and open the shutters to find her: under the shelves of the cupboard, a soda cracker softening in her mouth before she dared chew it; in the middle of her pallet, legs clenched tightly together to hold back her full bladder since a creaky floorboard separated her from the chamber pot.... There wasn't a speck of dirt in any of the rooms they boarded in, and they moved often. Sadie scraped the soles of her boots with sandpaper before she'd let herself into their room. The floor she kept bleached would have left telltale prints if she didn't. (66)

During all the time she is trying to be good, she keeps hoping that one day her mother will say to her, "I'm so proud of you. You are a good girl, Sadie" (68).

When Sadie turns thirteen, her mother commits some of the most atrocious crimes a mother can inflict on her own daughter: Not only does her mother sell her to men in the street, but a short time later, her mother takes her to a back-street doctor for an abortion and complete sterilization. Nevertheless, Sadie still believes that she should willingly obey her mother's commands because then this woman might love her.

Later, as a grown-up knowing that merely cleaning the kitchen will not create a miracle, Sadie develops some strange ideas about making her mother love her. For example, she fantasizes that she would "pick up a john who was old and very ugly. Maybe even deformed ... but ... also very rich. And he took her to this party and there were other old men there, just as deformed. One by one she took them, all day and all night, never resting, one by one. Two by two. Three by three" (70). Yet despite all her efforts, she never sees the fulfillment of her dream. It is only in her fantasies that her mother "would take one of the orchids and pin it on her collar and say, I knew you could do it. I'm so proud of you. You're a good girl" (871).

Although one day Sadie meets a man who marries her, her marriage does not turn into a happily-ever-after story but merely repeats her experience of denied love and affection. Like her mother, her husband is interested only in plenty of alcohol and a silent Sadie. The reader learns about Sadie's marriage:

> They ate their dinner totally in silence, unless it was one of those rare times he had a question to ask her or she had a repair for him to do. ... Sadie would fade into the corner chair as he drank while staring into the air. At first she'd tried reading; she liked picture books because her schooling didn't amount to a hill of beans and she could fill the missing story herself. But the house was so quiet he could still hear the pages turn. Noise, was all he had to say. She'd close the book in her lap. (81)

After her husband's death, Sadie receives the final blow to her miserable existence when her husband's two daughters want Sadie to pay $200 for a house that is a shack anyway. Since Sadie cannot come up with the money, she has to give in at last to poverty and homelessness. She realizes, "Dreams had been dying around [her] all of her life.... There were no more dreams" (97). As a homeless old woman, she, too, finally becomes an alcoholic and survives by selling her body to other junkies and to homeless men for twenty-five cents. This is her situation when she enters Bailey's café for the first time.

Like Sadie's life, Esther's destroyed life is also a product of the treatment she received from her immediate environment. When Bailey meets her for the first time, he is astonished at how much hatred one person alone is able to feel for the rest of the world. He observes that the "corner of the room was turned into a block of ice. It was hard to believe that someone's hate could change the air that way" (137). But if one learns about Esther's childhood, one understands her hatred. Growing up in a poor sharecropping family in the South, Esther is handed over as a twelve-year-old to her brother's white employer in whose basement she becomes a victim to his strange and unnatural sexual practices. As an exchange for this favor, Esther's brother gets higher wages with each passing year; because of his misused sister, he can now afford to buy convenient items such as "a Bendix washing machine" (143).

Esther, however, is not allowed to participate in this domestic bliss but has to meet her tormentor in his basement whenever he wants her there. These basement encounters have a devastating effect on Esther's self-esteem. She starts to believe that she is ugly and absolutely worthless as a woman because whenever she wonders why the man cannot meet her in a normal bedroom where he would be able to see her, she has to listen to his ideas about her: "The black gal. Monkey face. Tar. Coal. Ugly. Sot. Unspeakable. Pitch. Coal. Ugly. Soot. Unspeakable" (138). It does not take long for her to believe she is ugly; her destroyed self-esteem makes her say things like, "I am … glad that it is dark. He cannot see my face when he calls me to come down into the cellar" (138). In addition, Esther slowly begins to realize that nobody truly cares for her, but that everybody only misuses her for his or her egocentric desires. At first, she tries desperately to reconcile her innocent twelve-year-old's belief in brotherly love and love among married people with the things that have happened to her:

> This is your husband, my brother said. Do whatever he tells you, and you won't be sent away like the others. Can you be married without a gown? Without the beautiful white flowers and the veil that sweeps the floor of

> the church? Without love? Even at twelve years old I doubt, but I believe in my older brother. He is kind to me and calls me only *little sister.* (138)

Likewise, she tries to understand her relationship with her common-law husband after she has learned that the "leather and metal things [which] are small and sharp [and] greasy and smell funny" (141) serve his sadomasochistic appetite: "I try and try to find a word for what happens between us in the cellar. …my husband touches me and there are no babies. Is there another kind of touch? Should he touch me when I am in bed and not kneeling in the cellar?" (142). Eventually, however, she is able to clearly see herself as misused and betrayed by the people who were supposed to take care of her in the first place. After twelve years, she is finally able to leave her tormentor, yet she has turned into a person with no self-esteem and a tremendous hatred of men in general. This broken personality leads her to Bailey's café and Eve's house.

Unlike Sadie and Esther, Peaches has never had to experience the agonies of poverty and lovelessness in her life. Peaches comes from a middle-class home in Kansas City and grew up in a so-called functional family with her mother and father present throughout her childhood. But Naylor includes her to argue that even in such a stable environment, people are not protected from being able to destroy another person's life. At first, Peaches does not experience any evil intentions by other people during her childhood. On the contrary, her father is so excited about his little baby, "Daddy's beautiful baby" (148), that initially he has only love in mind. However, although her father's love starts out as normal, fatherly protection of a daughter because she is "his seventh child. The one daughter. The last is a father's gold" (148), as time passes, he becomes overly protective and obsessed with her. His initial love that caused him to make "a cotton sling to hang on his chest and [take her] everywhere" (148) turns into an obsession that makes him build a wall around the house when she turns nine and "prop his shotgun in full view" (149) if a boy attempts to socialize with her.

But it is not only her father's infatuation that hinders Peaches from developing a healthy personality. In addition, Peaches's spiritual development is destroyed by her neighbors, who watch the young girl's prettiness changing into adult beauty and immediately turn their envy into a righteous interpretation of a future downfall. Whereas the men still pretend to innocently admire her—her "father's friends would sit her on their knees, touch the soft curls on her head, raise her dimpled arms. The gal has promise, Jim" (151)—the women show their rejection more openly: "…the young and unmarried ones reflected her with an envy so intense it bordered on hate; those older and married, with a helpless fear" (150).

During her teenage years, Peaches comes to realize that everybody, including her own father, has created an alter ego for her. Because of her beauty, everybody expects her to act as a promiscuous woman. All her desperate efforts not to fit the image are in vain; she tells about her attempts:

> I tried everything to make her go away. I brought in straight A's at the academy. I worked part-time at the druggist's. I joined the Girl Guides. I joined the Missionary Circle. I rolled bandages for the resistance in Spain. I sang for the glee club. Sang for the war relief—sang in the church choir. But she was always there, reflected in the wetness of men's eyes. Tormenting me. I wore high-necked shirtwaists and loose skirts, thick woolen tights, even in the summertime, that scratched and left welts on my legs. But I could feel their eyes stripping my clothes away: they knew her promise was there. (152)

After being constantly confronted with her alter ego, she finally gives in to her negative image and turns herself into the person she never wanted to be in the first place but whom everybody expected her to be anyway. She freely and willingly allows every man to misuse her body for his personal sexual appetite, in "the cloak closets after school, behind the prayer altar, under the druggist's fountain, against the coal furnace in the Girls' Club, in the backs of milk wagons, in deserted streetcars, shadowed doorways. Any teacher. Any janitor. Any deacon.

Any porter. Any storekeeper. Any race, any age, any size—any son of any man" (152).

However, eventually she is no longer able to live in peace with her alter ego and begins to deeply hate herself: "I had only hated her [the alter ego]. Now I wanted to hate myself.... But it took a long time to hate myself as deeply as I wanted to hate" (155). Her self-hatred also causes her to brutally mutilate the right side of her face with a beer bottle opener. After a long and desperate journey throughout the United States, she finally reaches Eve's house because she has no more goals left for herself except to live out her self-hatred and her despair. As it has for all other characters in *Bailey's Café*, Naylor's street becomes for her the last possible place for survival.

Like Peaches, Jesse Bell finds first Bailey's café and then Eve's house because she has reached the lowest point in her self-destructiveness. She, too, had come to realize that her dreams and her reality were destroyed because of the people she had to live with. Originally from a rough working-class environment in Manhattan, Jesse Bell marries into Black high society. Yet from the very beginning, Jesse Bell is mistreated by her snobbish in-laws because of her working-class background; she observes, "Got it so when they mention my name up on Sugar Hill, noses flare out like they smelling something decayed. Oh yeah, Jesse Bell. The tramp from the docks. That slut who married into the King family" (170). The treatment by her in-laws, who cannot bear the fact that someone like Jesse Bell from a longshoremen background has entered their artificial world of pretended Black security and upper-class values with all their "upstanding Negroes, teachers, office clerks, doctors—educated folks" (170) eventually causes Jesse Bell to turn into a heroin addict.

With the story of the King family, Naylor closes her circle of criticizing every single class in society. While Sadie and Esther serve as examples for the lower class and Peaches for the middle class, Naylor uses Jesse Bell's case to criticize the Black upper class. Here, Naylor intends to especially reprove those members of the Black community who move up the career and social status ladders but disclaim at the same time their original backgrounds. Naylor criticizes them for trying to behave whiter than whites and deny everything connected to their Black past. For example, Jesse Bell observes that her husband refuses to eat dishes like "fried catfish … collard greens … biscuits … pork chops … macaroni salad with homemade mayonnaise … buttered cornbread … oxtail soup … sweet-potato pie" (178) because he was brought up believing that this was "slave food" (178). Every step the King family members take is dominated by their obsession that "[w]hite folks are looking at us. White folks are judging us" (181). Soon after marrying into their family, Jesse Bell finds out that the Kings' high-society behavior is merely social pretension because, on the one hand, they officially worship everything white and look down on every activity that might be connected to Black lower-class behavior, and, on the other hand, they secretly show up at Jesse Bell's house to play cards, listen to jazz, learn all the new and hot dances, and drink Jack Daniel's the whole night long. As for respect and love for each other, Jesse Bell observes that most of their emotions are merely a big show, too, serving only to act out high society. For example, Jesse Bell watches some of the worst treatments of women:

> Those women got treated any old way and took it. I don't mean being slapped upside the head or any such thing … there are worse things than hitting a woman. Like having your husband call you stupid and lazy in front of a roomful of people while you stand there and smile and smile. No, the man wouldn't use the words *stupid* or *lazy*, but it amounted to the same thing. And if I could figure it out with my lack of education, surely she could, and still she smiles and smiles and smiles. Yeah, they are worse things. Like having the girlfriend and the wife at the same dinner table. Like the wife knowing about it all the while, and the husband knowing she knows, and him getting a thrill out of it all. Cause the wife's not going to say a word. Cause this son of a bitch is a doctor somebody or a lawyer somebody—or maybe just a man somebody she feels she's nobody without. Women up there look at other women as nothing unless they're attached to some man's name. And attached they stay, no matter what he does. And personally, I knew a few of them who actually got their butts beaten worse than some women down on the docks. But they got beaten

> by stone sober men behind stained-glass doors. And with all their money, they couldn't afford to cry. (175)

The Kings' willingness to sacrifice everything to social status slowly ruins Jesse Bell. Uncle Eli, the family's oldest member and tyrant, especially resents the fact that someone "as low" as Jesse Bell could enter his family. Therefore, he wants to make sure that Jesse Bell's son does not even think about the Bells as family, but only as people with whom one has no desire to socialize. When her son is born, Jesse Bell is confronted with Uncle Eli's decision to bring him up in the high-society spirit. Jesse Bell tells about the conflict:

> I wanted Mother to live in and help take care of the baby.... Uncle Eli wanted a nanny. I wanted him to go to school with the other kids in the neighborhood, so he could play stickball, get the regular ruckus that boys do, and learn to take his knocks. Uncle Eli wanted a private tutor. (183)

This conflict continues throughout the boy's childhood and teenage years. Every incident in his life is dominated by Uncle Eli's obsession with reminding Jesse Bell that her working-class background is a shame to the family. She is not allowed to decide anything, such as "what friends should come to his birthday parties, what clothes he should take to camp, what books he should read" (184). In the end, Uncle Eli's efforts indeed pay off because when Jesse Bell's mother celebrates her ninetieth birthday, Jesse Bell's son refuses to go because he does not "have anything in common with *those people*" (184). At this point Jesse Bell finally gives in to Uncle Eli and concludes that he succeeded in "kill[ing] me. He was a murderer—a cold-blooded murderer ... he took my husband and son. And they were all I lived for" (170). As a result, she turns to heroin, from which she can free herself only after living with Eve.

In addition to these women's stories, Naylor includes the story of Miss Maple, a Black man with a Ph.D. in statistics from Stanford University. Whereas all her women's stories allow Naylor to criticize the way people in general live with each other, Miss Maple's story criticizes white American racist society.

Miss Maple is not the typical Black male one expects to find in contemporary Black women's literature. Originally named Stanley Beckwourth Booker T. Washington Carver, he comes from a proud background and a successful African American business family that has been prosperous for several generations; his father alone inherited from his own father 3,000 acres of "some of the richest land in Imperial Valley" (238) in southern California. However, when living in Eve's house, he voluntarily does the lowest work such as cleaning the house for all the other women. Yet the really interesting thing that strikes one immediately about him is not his work but his appearance since he wears women's clothing. It is important to understand that even though Miss Maple dresses like a woman, he is not a homosexual or a cross-dresser, but a heterosexual man who also perceives himself as one. Bailey reports about Miss Maple's appearance:

> We're talking no wigs. We're talking no makeup. No padded falsies. No switching. And if it's near the evening, we're talking a five o'clock shadow that he runs his hands over like any tired man after a day of hard work.... He'll straddle the counter stool like a man, order in a deep voice, and eat his meal in a no-nonsense fashion. (233)

His cross-dressing is the final, frustrated outcome of a long and disappointing job search throughout the United States. During this journey he realizes that the white males who occupy the executive positions in the business world will always make sure that their power will never be shared with a Black man. He started his job search because his original dream was to open his own marketing firm, and the first step in that direction would be to "earn [his] own money" (281). Yet although he is a straight-A Ph.D. from Stanford, he is turned down during every single interview. After ninety-nine interviews with different companies, he has seen the full amount of racial discrimination in the American executive world.

On the one hand, he is confronted with the typical stereotypes about Black people and their abilities; e.g., many executives have a hard time imagining a Black person with a Ph.D. from Stanford, not to mention the fact that his family owns about 3,000 acres of land in California and are well-to-do business people. Some of these executives feel a bit better when they learn that at least the family "grow[s] cotton on the farm" (237). On the other hand, he realizes that under no circumstances will an executive even consider a Black person for an upper-level position. During many interviews Miss Maple can see that "they kept reading and rereading my college transcripts, flipping through the charts—God, how they could use someone like this, *needed* someone like this—and then the shattered hopes when they finally looked back at me and a different man hadn't materialized in front of them" (282). In the end, after all those interviews, he has been offered only positions as "head custodian" (237) or "bellboy, mailroom clerk, sleeping-car porter, elevator operator" (238).

Although his cross-dressing comes as a result of his realization of the racial discrimination during all those interviews, it first happens more as an accident, not as a deliberate act. While in Pittsburgh during some very hot summer days, he exchanges his "Wall Street banker" (235) outfit, the expected clothing for a position he is dreaming about, with a comfortable summer dress, which makes it easier for him to deal with the hot summer weather. Soon, however, after being turned down again for another possible job, he begins to wonder whether a Black man will always be turned down for an executive position simply because people in power are too afraid to share this power with a Black person. Therefore, he conducts an experiment by wearing female business attire for his interviews.

Indeed, his cross-dressing for his interviews proves what he already suspects: It does not make a difference whether a Black man wears an expensive gray flannel suit and a vest, the power outfit for the executive world, or whether a man wears women's attire because the reaction is always exactly the same; people "stared" (291), had a "shock on their faces" (289), and gave him "frightened glances" (291). Until that realization, he had always hoped that perhaps the next interview would bring the job offer. But now, the cross dressing helps him see that the white business world in general does not have a place for a Black person. Their racism is a universal and not an isolated phenomenon. Therefore, he gives up his dream and instead adopts a completely nihilistic attitude. When he finally reaches Gabe's pawnshop, he is "set on using the last money he had in his pocket to buy a pawnshop revolver—and just one bullet" (235).

Bloch claims that concrete utopian texts can provide political inspiration for the reader if they describe the Faustian representatives' journeys to "free ground," depicting first the protagonists' personal development toward self-empowerment and change-willing attitudes and then the protagonists' personal involvement in transforming communities. In my analysis of *Bailey's Café*, I have shown so far that Naylor's characters suffer so much from their own pain and lost dreams that when they arrive in Naylor's street, they have no concern for their communities' changes; their preoccupation with their own despair has caused them to be completely powerless. An application of concrete utopian ideas to these characters would imply that they need to develop enough distance from their own suffering and recover enough strength to go back to their respective realities where they can recognize and execute changes. Naylor fulfills this Blochian requirement, for she allows her characters to go through a transitional time of healing and self-empowerment. She matches Bloch's idea about sending individuals on spiritual journeys because she allows her characters not just turn themselves over to nihilism and despair but to learn to work actively on changing circumstances for themselves. For example, before sending all her other protagonists on their spiritual journeys, Naylor sends Eve, after the departure from her stepfather, on a dangerous trip through the Louisiana delta, and when

Eve finally arrives near New Orleans more dead than alive, Naylor has her reminisce about her life choices:

> And when I finally reached Arabi, dead lice and gnats in my matted hair, the flour sack a filthy remnant of strings and twigs, mettles buried into the caked mud on my ankles, I sank to my knees to think. Ten miles outside New Orleans. By then I'd lived a hundred years ten times over, so there was a lot to think about. I'd paid for this ordeal with a loss of good eyesight and a loss of sense of humor.... And the only road that lay open to me was the one ahead, and the only way I could walk it was the way I was. *I had no choice but to walk into New Orleans neither male nor female—mud. But I could right then and there choose what I was going to be when I walked back out.*[100] (133)

Eve's choice of what she is going to be when she will leave New Orleans represents her Blochian vision, her glimpse of the *not-yet-become*. Guided by her vision throughout her time in New Orleans, she indeed succeeds in determining her own circumstances. The reader learns about Eve's departure from New Orleans:

> I carried into New Orleans poor eyesight, no sense of humor, and a body of mud. I was ready to leave ten years later with the three steamer trunks of imported silk suits, not one of them brown; fifty-seven thousand, six hundred and forty-one dollars, not one of them earned on my back; and a love of well-kept gardens. (133)

In the same way Eve overcomes a disastrous background by having a vision of a better future, Naylor provides all the women in Eve's boardinghouse and some people in Bailey's café with a vision and enables them to act accordingly. To help them in this process, Naylor uses her nonrealistic street as the transitional space where her characters can gain this vision and turn despair into hope. In every single case, be it Sadie, Esther, Peaches, Jesse Bell, or Miss Maple, one can see the healing process taking place because of Naylor's street.

---

[100] Italics are mine—H. R.-H.

Sadie, for example, who throughout her entire life has been desperately hoping someone would truly love her, finally finds this love in Bailey's café. Until this point, she has lived with the attitude of "very very good was to be deserving of the love she believed was waiting in return" (67), an attitude she developed because of her disastrous childhood. This attitude has determined her way of dealing with the people in her immediate environment all her life and has caused her to turn herself into a voiceless being without any self-esteem. Even her price as a prostitute displays her suffering self-esteem. Every day she asks only for the missing amount for one bottle of wine and some days that might just be "2 or 3 cents" (102), but this causes men to turn her down because "they'd gladly have taken her if she'd asked for much more" (192).

Because of Bailey's café, she experiences for the first time in her life that someone is interested in her comments, her ideas, and, especially, her laughter. Iceman Jones, another customer at Bailey's, is first moved by Sadie because he "met the eyes of a four-year-old dreaming to survive" (105). But he honestly falls in love with her when he hears her laughter after he tells one of his famous stories. Since it is the very first time that Sadie laughs, Bailey recalls the incident: "...the whole café stood still. In the presence of something that beautiful and rare, you're afraid to move, afraid to breathe. ...none of us, especially Jones, would ever be the same again" (109). Jones is so moved that he invites Sadie for a dance in the void where she receives her first kiss; in addition, Jones offers her marriage. The awareness of his love enables Sadie to find her own self-love and self-esteem; because of his love, she is able to develop the necessary distance from her own self. Instead of measuring her self-worth according to the love she receives from others, she is now able to realize that the most important form of love is self-love. With such a healed personality, she is able to understand that she does not need to enslave herself any longer to the people whose love she has been desperately hoping to win as she did with her mother and her husband. No longer does she have to give up all of her own dreams for another person because of her missing self-esteem. As a consequence of her new self-love and self-respect, she is able to reject Iceman Jones's offer of marriage and go back to her life as a poor, but independent, person.

Likewise, Esther, Peaches, and Jesse Bell receive the chance of healing and self-empowerment in Naylor's street. These three, however, experience their healing process in Eve's boardinghouse-bordello, where they can rest and rethink options for themselves while Eve serves as their catalyst. For Esther and Peaches, Naylor offers some interesting healing methods. Esther, for instance, who was forced to perform sadomasochistic acts in a dark basement for twelve years, now performs these same acts in Eve's dark basement, but this time it is completely Esther's own decision. She chooses to perform those acts in Eve's house because for her healing process it is important to lavish her hatred on all men to purify her emotions. Here in Eve's house, she is also the one who sets the rules for the game; for instance, she admits only customers who "bring me the white roses. And they must call me *little sister*" (144). Relishing in her hatred and finally receiving the white roses she never got for a proper wedding help her eventually to perceive herself as a woman with dignity and virtue.

Similarly, Naylor offers a strange method of healing and self-empowerment for Peaches. Before Peaches found Eve's house, her greatest problem was that she could not develop any love or respect for herself because, from the time she was a little girl, everybody merely loved her beauty but was not interested in her as a whole person. Consequently, such missing love caused her to develop an emotionally dead personality. Because of her missing self-love and self-respect, she has never been able to experience a true love relationship, either as a daughter, sister, friend, or lover, but has only offered her body for use by anyone. In Eve's house, Peaches learns to develop an intact personality that allows her to gain emotions such as self-respect and self-love. As in Esther's case, Eve encourages Peaches to take the same method that at first had a destroying effect on her and to use it now as a healing device. For Peaches, Eve's idea implies that Peaches admit as many customers as possible. The reader learns that men "sit knee to knee in the parlor … [because] the word didn't take long to spread. The hot one who moved into the second-floor room takes on all callers" (163). However, now her sexual encounters differ from the ones in her past because Eve encourages her to "look in that mirror good and accept no less than what you deserve" (164). This time, Peaches learns not to have "quickies" with someone but to spend time with a man and make him appreciate her as a complete woman with many different sides, not merely a physical one. By doing so, Peaches experiences herself as a spiritual person, thus slowly developing self-respect. When her father shows up at Eve's house because he wants to take her home, Eve promises him, "I'll return your daughter to you whole" (165). Eve's promise shows that Peaches is a Blochian person *en route* who one day will have found her own *ultimate true human identity*.

Jesse Bell, too, is a Faustian representative who finds her *ultimate true human identity* in Eve's house. In Jesse Bell's story the reader is able to observe in a superb way Bloch's requirement for a vision that initiates changes because Jesse Bell is able to give up her heroin addiction after she has a vision of herself as a still-innocent young girl. At first she tries several times to overcome her addiction without that vision. However, all her attempts are in vain because without the vision, she has not yet developed a true *change-willing attitude*. Therefore, she repeats the same pattern every single time she has just survived another attempt to give up her addiction: As soon as she gets offered some fresh heroin with all the necessary utensils, Jesse Bell goes straight back to her addiction. Even her decision to go "cold turkey," which she describes as "pieces of your skull stabbing back into your brain, your lungs collapsing in, each bone snapping and crumbling, your insides busting open as your guts rip apart" (199), does not help her adopt the truly *change-willing attitude* that Bloch claims can be developed only if one has a vision.

Eve, however, knows about the necessity of the Blochian vision because after watching Jesse Bell go through the living hell of the "cold turkey" method several times, she takes Jesse Bell to Bailey's void. There Jesse Bell sees herself one more time during her innocent childhood, together with her dreams about her adult future:

> And there it was: the simple bedroom she'd had as a girl. The raw pine floor. The single window looking out at other tar-paper shacks on the waterfront. Her bed with the chenille spread. Her secondhand dresser. Her movie-star posters torn from *Modern Screen* and tacked on the mildewed wall: Bette Davis. Irene Dunn. Clark Gable. Joan Crawford. She could even hear Mother wrestling with that old wood stove in the kitchen, smell the frying butterfish and turnip greens. A lump formed in her throat.... That's when she saw the rosewood rocker and matching chest in the corner ... the top opening up to reveal neat stacks of thick cotton towels and beige sheets. A small door led into a bathroom: a claw-foot tub with gleaming faucets shaped like swans, cool blue tiles underfoot, scented French soap in porcelain trays, crystal jars of bath salts sparkling on the windowsill.
>
> —I dreamed of a bathroom like this when I was a little girl. (198)

When Jesse Bell recognizes the beautiful bathroom she used to dream about, she realizes that her current life does not match her earlier dreams. Her old dream becomes her new vision, providing her with the necessary strength to eventually give up her heroin addiction for good. Bailey testifies to the truly free Jesse Bell every time she visits his café when he comments on the "healthy tones of her skin" (190) and describes her laughter as "good-natured and com[ing] from deep down" (169).

Like Jesse Bell, Miss Maple, too, heals because of the vision he receives in the void of Bailey' café. Before his spiritual breakdown he had inherited a dream from his Native American grandmother, whose entire life was directed by her vision of *Ha lup* (snow) in the desert. *Ha lup* in the desert, which made her dream about her sons' future—"And I saw my sons, dark as the night, proud as the eagles, picking white gold from the land" (279)—also led to the family's tremendous wealth. This grandmother, a truly Blochian representative, taught her offspring the necessity of a dream that will inspire.

The idea of *Ha lup* in the desert had already helped Miss Maple through a difficult time in jail as a conscientious objector; he recalls later, "After they called lights-out and the pain soared beyond the reach of my Christian prayers, [*Ha lup*] became a mantra to replace all of the discarded reasons for my having chosen not to die" (280). This same vision of *Ha lup* in the desert inspires him when he starts out on his journey through the United States in search of a job as a financial analyst. However, since his search turns out differently than he had expected, he loses his faith in his grandmother's vision. As I discussed earlier in this chapter, he expresses his loss of hope and vision by wearing women's attire.

To understand why Naylor makes Miss Maple take to cross-dressing, one can turn to bell hooks, who explains the dilemma of many Black men in a white supremacist racist society. She shows how racist patriarchal power affects Black male self-esteem:

> Many heterosexual black men in white supremacist patriarchal culture have acted as though the primary "evil" of racism has been the refusal of the dominant culture to allow the full access to patriarchal power, so that in sexist terms they are compelled to inhabit a sphere of powerlessness, deemed "feminine," hence they have perceived themselves as emasculated. To the extent that black men accept a white supremacist sexist representation of themselves as castrated, without phallic power, and therefore pseudo-females, they will need to overly assert a phallic misogynist masculinity, one rooted in contempt for the female.[101]

In *Bailey's Café*, Naylor takes the Black male contempt for the feminine and makes it part of the healing process. If Miss Maple wants to be a man walking upright again, he has to reconcile himself with the hostile feminine side. Only by doing so will he be able to eventually find peace and hope again and fully accept

---

[101] bell hooks, *Black Looks. Race and Representation* (Boston: South End Press, 1992) 147.

his Black masculinity in white America. Therefore, he lives in Eve's women's-only boardinghouse and does stereotypical low women's work such as cleaning.

After his contemplative stay at Eve's house, where he, too, receives the chance to pause and rethink his life, he is finally brave enough to allow his grandmother's vision to become his own dream again. It is in Bailey's void where he learns to dream anew; Bailey watches him:

> [Miss Maple] takes his full champagne glass to the rear of the café. …he steps off boldly into the midst of nothing and is suspended midair by a gentle wind that starts to swirl his cape around his knees. It's a hot, dry wind that could easily have been born in a desert, but it's bringing, of all things, snow. Soft and silent it falls, coating his shoulders, his upturned face. Snow. He holds his glass up and turns to me as a single flake catches on the rim before melting down the side into an amber world where bubbles burst and are born, burst and are born. (309)

Because the rediscovered vision of *Ha lup* in the desert helps Miss Maple regain his belief in his own abilities, he is now able to go back to his original world. Therefore, he decides that at the end of the next year he will return to reality and pursue his original dream of starting his own marketing company.

In addition to the portrayal of the Faustian representatives' development toward *walking upright*, Bloch's theory asks for some form of community change. Since Bloch is not interested in merely some personal psychological writing but in the changed human society, he requires that a concrete utopian text depict some form of a community change to provide political inspiration for the reader. In regard to *Bailey's Café*, it seems at first that Naylor fails Bloch's specific requirement, for she does not present any of her characters in a poststreet reality. However, the description of any form of a post-street reality would not work with *Bailey's Café* anyway because Naylor's interest lies in creating a symbolic nonreality. But looking at her symbolic nonreality, one recognizes that she fulfills the specific Blochian requirement of community change.

Since Naylor's thesis was that ordinary people cannot live together in peace because they cause each other pain and despair, a community change in *Bailey's Café* must portray all the different individuals as allowing each other enough space for differences while still having great respect for each other, thus regarding each other as equally important human beings. To help this group of people begin to practice livable community with each other, Naylor uses a unique method: She has the Messiah being born again, this time in Bailey's café in the middle of the twentieth century. To achieve this, she lets one of her characters, Mary, a Black thirteen-year-old Jewish virgin from Ethiopia, have a baby boy named George. Similar to the miracle of Bethlehem, everybody in the café sees a great lighting going off when Mary's baby is born:

> Sparkling. Shimmering. Waves of light. We could see them even from the front of the café.... Silvers. Pearls. Iridescent pinks. They now sprayed out into the sunless room and hit the ceiling. The walls. The floor. Glowing copper. Gilded orange. And all kinds of gold. Sequins of light that swirled and spun through the air. Cascades of light flowing in, breaking up, ad rolling like fluid diamonds over the worn tile. Emerald. Turquoise. Sapphire. It went on for hours. (321)

Yet in contrast to the Biblical messiah who comes to desperate people to liberate them, Naylor's messiah presents a Blochian messiah: He comes to desperate people, too, but when he arrives, they have already liberated themselves from their pain and despair through a process of self-empowerment. Maxine Lavon Montgomery states that "in what is an original revision of the classic Christmas story, the text culminates with a portrait of a radically transformed society where all externally imposed limitations and labels are blurred."[102]

But the messiah is still necessary because, like the Biblical messiah's arrival, Baby George's arrival signals the beginning of a new era. In *Bailey's Café* it means that a group of people who have never experienced the concept of a

---

[102] Maxine Lavon Montgomery, "Authority, Multivocality, and the New World Order in Gloria Naylor's *Bailey's Café*," *African American Review* 29.1 (1995): 31.

livable community before have now healed to such a degree that they can try out community together. Similar to the very first church of the New Testament, Baby George's birth has caused all of them, regardless of their gender, race, class, or religious or ethnic background, to come together for the very first time. Even someone like Esther, who never leaves her basement at Eve's house and hates men so much that she does not even allow Miss Maple to come into her room to clean, "squeez[es] herself into the darkest corner of the room, sitting on the floor with her arms wrapped around her knees. But even her face [is] in awe" (321). Everybody else is dancing; Bailey and Miss Maple, who normally have a hard time liking Gabe, the Jew, hold hands with him while dancing together, and Esther, the men-hater, is smiling while watching the three men dancing. Peaches, who hardly ever talks, starts singing and "one voice joined in. Another voice joined. And another" (322) until finally the whole group is singing, "a bit ragged and off-key. But all singing" (323).

In her discussion of *Bailey's Café*, Virginia Fowler points to a crucial aspect of Peaches's song. Peaches's line "Anybody Ask You Who You Are" is the first line of a spiritual that ends with "Tell him—you're the child of God." Since they all join Peaches in singing her song, this indicates, according to Fowler, that even if the world or they themselves have defined their own personalities as dysfunctional and thus they were not worthy to be anybody's children, they have now learned to accept themselves—the world might not accept them, but God did.[103]

But the highlight of their celebration of community occurs at Baby George's circumcision ceremony. Naylor designs the scene as a truly multicultural ceremony. Here, during the ceremony, all different groups realize together that life is a "ceremony about survival" (323). Therefore, to survive, they should not use differences against one another. This knowledge helps them overcome, at least in their small world in Bailey's café, all cultural and national

[103] Fowler, "A Conversation with Gloria Naylor," 139.

separations that have caused the world to fight since its beginning. For instance, Gabe can live with the idea that two heathen brothers, Miss Maple and Bailey, can join him in one of the holiest ceremonies for Jewish people. Bailey reports, "I had to stand in as the honorary *sandek*, the godfather. And Miss Maple took the role of the other male guests to help me respond to the blessing. Don't worry, Gabe said; God will forgive you for not being Jews" (323). Rebecca Wood points out that with the circumcision ceremony, Naylor "destabilizes the universal and national perspectives in an effort to construct a liberated view which allows for cultural difference while recognizing that difference within a pluralist universal community."[104]

With Baby George's circumcision ceremony, Naylor's people prove that they can function as a community—not a perfect one, but one where individuals can at last live in human dignity, receive and pay respect and have a realistic hope to fulfill their respective dreams. Bailey sums it all up when he claims, "Nothing important can happen unless they're all in it together as a community" (324). Naylor's Faustian representatives will eventually go back to reality, but this time they will take the experienced spirit of potential community with them to their particular old or new places, and their new knowledge will help them successfully face future challenges.

---

[104] Rebecca S. Wood, "'Two Warring Ideals in One Dark Body': Universalism and Nationalism in Gloria Naylor's *Bailey's Café*," *African American Review* 30.3 (Fall 1996): 393.

Chapter 4

A Revival of Ancestral Hope

Julie Dash's *Daughters of the Dust*

In my previous chapters, I applied my Blochian thesis to novels. However, in my introduction I claim that Bloch's ideas work not only for fiction but also for films produced by contemporary African American women artists. Therefore, in this chapter I will analyze a movie produced by a Black woman according to its ability to transmit *anticipatory illumination* and concrete utopian hope to its African American audience. I have chosen film producer Julie Dash's second movie, *Daughters of the Dust*, which was released in 1991. As in *Beloved* and *Bailey's Café*, in *Daughters* one can also observe Faustian representatives *en route* toward their ultimate true human identity. Here, too, people learn to empower themselves because of a vision or an enabling daydream they have had; as a result of their revolutionary *forward dreaming*, they begin, step by step, to change their personal circumstances.

As I argued, art that can be considered a Blochian concrete utopia always intends to motivate its recipients toward their own political agency. Bloch's concept of the political motivation matches Dash's expectations for *Daughters* in superb ways as Dash allows her protagonists to receive "glimpses of the eternal" (133),[105] an idea that equals Bloch's glimpses of the *not-yet-become*. Although the setting of the movie is 1902 and seems at first to be unrelated to the Black community of the 1990s, Dash nevertheless deals in *Daughters* with problems that, according to her, Black people still face today in American society. Like Walker, Morrison, and Naylor, Dash hopes to influence contemporary African Americans toward questioning current attitudes and circumstances and consider possible changes. In fact, Dash even claims that one of her main objectives with *Daughters* was to influence her own community toward political agency. In her interview with bell hooks, she agrees with hooks that the film intends "progressive political intervention."[106] In line with Bloch's audience inspiration, she argues that *Daughters* should be able to succeed in regard to its political intention because in this movie the spectators "are inside; we're right in there."[107]

To understand Dash's contemporary plea, one should look first at the historical setting of *Daughters*. The film takes place on a small island off the Atlantic coast of South Carolina. Here we meet an African American extended family, the Peazants, on the eve of their departure from the sea island in the South to a big city in the North. Everybody in the family believes that the move up North will improve living conditions. Nana, the 88-year-old great-grandmother of the Peazant family, is the only one who realizes that a geographic relocation will not bring the ultimate happiness the Peazant members dream about because one of their main problems is that they have lost their sense of unity and identity as an African American group. Nana sees that many family members have only their

---

[105] All references to *Daughters of the Dust* in this chapter will be given in parentheses in the text and will be cited from the following edition: Julie Dash, Screenplay, *Daughters of the Dust. The Making of an African American Woman's Film* (New York: The New Press, 1992) 73-164.

[106] Julie Dash, "Dialogue between bell hooks and Julie Dash," *Daughters of the Dust. The Making of an African American Woman's Film* (New York: The New Press, 1992) 32.

[107] Julie Dash, "Dialogue between bell hooks and Julie Dash," 33.

own, egocentric desires in mind when they dream about the North. In addition, they disrespect and degrade each other instead of working together. Most of them have either forgotten about their unique African American heritage and history or reject those parts of themselves out of embarrassment.

Their attitudes, however, have now led them to an obsession with Western or mainstream American ideas, such as placing materialistic desires over spiritual well-being. They have completely lost the spirit of their ancestors, who knew they could survive in hostile white American society only if they lived together in unity and envisioned a common future for all of them. Nana understands that her family members will not have the necessary strength to face racist, sexist, and economic exploitation in the North if they do not rediscover their ancestors' spirit while still on the island.

Nana's hopes and fears for her family mirror Julie Dash's own hopes and fears for the contemporary African American community: The same way Nana sees that her family needs to rediscover its ancestors' ability to envision a future together as a group, contemporary African Americans have to discover their ancestors' ideas about unity. As Cornel West argues in his *Race Matters*, today many African Americans have lost a sense of unity among themselves and have fallen apart into many different groups that work against, instead of with, each other.[108] Even the class system of bourgeoisie society has entered the African American group and divided its members into all classes, be it under, low, middle, or upper, that have antagonistic relationships with one another.

With *Daughters*, Dash intends to convey to her own African American people in the 1990s that the strength they need for survival in a society that is still hostile to them lies in each other and in their unity. She believes that if Black people really want to succeed in changing American society, they should not drown themselves in Western materialistic and egocentric attitudes, but should

---

[108] For West's argument, see especially his chapter on Black leadership in his *Race Matters*: Cornel West, "The Crisis of Black Leadership," *Race Matters* (Boston: Beacon Press, 1993) 33-46.

start again to appreciate themselves as a community. They should realize again their uniqueness as a group by remembering their recent African American history, their ancient African heritage, and the beauty and richness of their own culture.

In his discussion of *Daughters*, Manthia Diawara explains that the movie urges African Americans in the 1990s "to know where we came from, before knowing where we are going."[109] And Toni Cade Bambara supports Diawara's thesis when she claims about the movie's potential that "the film, in fact, invites the spectator to undergo a triple process of recollecting the dismembered past, recognizing and reappraising cultural icons and codes, and recentering and revalidating the self."[110]

Dash's invitation to her audience to identify with the protagonists meets Bloch's concrete utopian theory which, too, invites readers to identity with Faustian representatives in order to find visions for their own realities. For my Blochian discussion of Dash's movie, I will concentrate on Bloch's aspect of the mere longing and the enabling daydream because here in *Daughters*, Bloch's daydream theory is applied to a work of art in an excellent way.[111] As I argue, the main objective in *Daughters* is connected to the Peazants' search for their ancestors' spirit before their departure to the North. When one analyzes the family's efforts to reach its ancestors' communal awareness, it is obvious that the

---

[109] Manthia Diawara, "Black American Cinema: The New Realism," *Black American Cinema,* ed. Manthia Diawara (New York: Routledge, 1993) 14.

[110] Toni Cade Bambara, "Reading the Signs, Empowering the Eye," *Black American Cinema,* ed. Manthia Diawara (New York: Routledge, 1993) 124.

[111] A reading of Joel Brouwer's analysis of *Daughters of the Dust* would offer an additional focus for a possible Blochian interpretation. In his discussion, Brouwer calls the Unborn Child a not-yet-born character, a concept that, according to him, could call for further interpretation. The *not-yet* is indeed a major aspect of Bloch's theory, and one could also take Brouwer's idea as an invitation to read the text under the aspect of the *not-yet-become*. See Joel R. Brouwer, "Repositioning: Center and Margin in Julie Dash's *Daughters of the Dust,*" *African American Review* 29.1 (1995): 10.

text clearly invites an application of Bloch's daydream ideas. Therefore, before discussing the movie, one should look again at Bloch's daydream theory.

I showed earlier that Bloch distinguishes between two daydreams, the dream that implies only mere longing, thus providing an escape from reality but not enabling the dreamer to become active, and the dream that provides a vision of changed societal conditions, thus enabling the dreamer to work actively against unsatisfactory circumstances. Whereas the first dream presents simply an exercise in escapism, the second epitomizes hope and contains Bloch's specific *revolutionary forward dreaming*. If an individual is *revolutionary forward dreaming* and not *merely longing*, "the weary, weakening quality that can be characteristic of mere longing then disappears; on the contrary, longing now shows what it can really do.... It is capable of revolutionary consciousness, it can climb into the carriage of history."[112]

In association with his ideas about daydreams, Bloch analyzes filled and expectant emotions. People who *merely long* are driven by filled emotions like envy, greed, or admiration, which "are those whose drive-intention is short-term, whose drive-object lies ready, if not in individual attainability, then in the already available world."[113] In comparison, people who *revolutionary forward dream* live with expectant emotions. According to Bloch, "Expectant emotions (like anxiety, fear, hope, belief), on the other hand, are those whose drive-intention is long-term, whose drive-object does not yet lie ready, not just in individual attainability, but also in the already available world, and therefore still occurs in the doubt about exit or entrance."[114] As I explained earlier, to illustrate his point, Bloch uses the example of the hungry person: Whereas filled emotions would cause a hungry person to search for food immediately within the old framework, expectant

---

[112] Bloch, *Principle*, 1365.

[113] Bloch, *Principle*, 74.

[114] Bloch, *Principle*, 74.

emotions would cause the person to seek to change the situation that caused hunger in the first place.

In *Daughters*, Bloch's two categories of the daydream are superbly executed. The movie starts out with most family members having dreams about the North. These dreams belong to Bloch's first dream category, and most are connected to materialistic things. The family members hope for material possessions, higher-paying jobs, and better education for their children, which in turn will provide them later with better economic conditions. They entertain themselves with a mail-order Sears Roebuck catalogue, telling each other about the items they would like to order in the future: "I wish I had this doll … I wish I had this bed to go inside my house … I wish I had a house" (134). As Bloch claims about the filled emotions, the Peazants wish only for the immediate fulfillment of their self-centered desires without any understanding of the racist and sexist structures of their society.

Other members' dreams are not materialistic; however, their dreams are as naïve as the materialistic ones. Consequently, their dreams, too, belong to the first Blochian category connected to filled emotions. Viola, for example, one of the granddaughters who left the island years ago, returns now as a reborn Christian with a missionary dream for her family. She is glad that the family is moving north because she hopes that everybody will find Christianity and middle-class values. Her missionary dream for her family comes as an immediate result of her attitude toward her own culture; she serves as a representative of the group of Black people who, out of embarrassment about their own culture, readily accept every Western cultural system, at the same time completely discarding their own culture without even considering whether it was indeed inferior to the Western one. Viola's embarrassment becomes obvious when she gives her friend, Mr. Snead, a photographer from Philadelphia, her opinion about the family's departure day: "I see this day as their first steps towards progress, an engraved invitation, you might say, to the culture, education and wealth of the mainland" (79).

To speed up the family's process of adapting to the new culture, she starts Sunday school lessons right there on the beach, informing everybody, "When I left these islands, I was a sinner and I didn't even know it. But I left these islands, touched that mainland, and fell into the arms of the Lord" (115). In addition, she teaches her younger family members some middle-class values. For instance, she holds etiquette classes for the female teenagers, at which she instructs them how to sit ladylike on a chair with crossed legs and how to walk decently without running or showing any excitement.

Haagar, one of Nana's granddaughters-in-law, represents another example of a Peazant whose dreams result from total embarrassment about her own culture. In Haagar's understanding, happiness and fulfilled lives for her three children can happen only after a complete denial of all ancestral values and belief systems. Therefore, she dreams of leaving all the "Hoodoo mess" behind when they move north; she summarizes her dream, "Those old people, they pray to the sun, they pray to the moon … sometimes just to a big start! They ain't got no religion in them. No! This is a new world we're moving into, and I want my daughters to grow up to be decent 'somebodies'" (131).

Yellow Mary, one of the Peazants who left many years ago and returns now to attend the reunion, dreams another egocentric, but also very lonely, dream. Since she experiences a tremendous amount of ostracism and hatred by her own family because she has returned as a prostitute, her dream is to live in a far-away place like Nova Scotia without having any contact with her family at all. Although she does not even know the place, Nova Scotia seems like paradise to her because the foreign sound of the name alone promises enough distance from her family and, consequently, hope for her dream's fulfillment.

And Eli, one of Nana's grandsons, announces publicly, "I ain't got no more dreams" (132), but he dreams secretly about personal male revenge before his departure to the North. His revenge dreams result from the rape of his wife, Eula. Since that day he has claimed that he does not dream about anything anymore, for his problem is that his wife refuses to divulge the name of her rapist, a white man. She does so not because she wants to protect the rapist but because she wants to protect Eli himself. She knows that Eli would not have the slightest chance of avenging his pride as a Black man in Southern white society without getting lynched. Still, the only thing on Eli's mind is his quick revenge so he can reestablish his male pride before moving to the North. Because Eula refuses to cooperate with him, he considers himself more betrayed and hurting than she is. Consequently, instead of supporting her in her own agony, he treats her with tremendous disgust and contempt and behaves toward her as if she herself is to blame for the rape, leaving her completely alone in her pain about her sexual misuse. He tells Nana, "I don't feel like she's mine anymore. When I look at her, I feel I don't want her anymore" (95). Because of his hurt pride, he not only rejects Eula but also the child, the Unborn Child, she is carrying. Although she repeatedly tells him that the child is his, he is made so blind by his male pride complex that he refuses to acknowledge her child as his. Eli's secret revenge dream serves as an example of Bloch's idea of the *mere longing* dream connected to filled emotions. As Bloch's theory claims, Eli has only his immediate satisfaction based on spontaneous emotions in mind, without considering any long-term consequences for him or his wife.

As I already argued, all these Peazants' dreams belong to Bloch's first category of daydreaming, the *mere longing* dream connected to filled emotions. Although nothing is wrong in dreaming up future wish fulfillments, the problem is that their filled emotions make the Peazants so blind that they believe that Northern society will be racist- and sexist-free. They think that as long as they leave the island and move up North, everything will be better for them. It does not occur to them at all that American society in general, Northern and Southern, needs changes in regard to the African American situation. They do not realize that they themselves would have to be the ones to work on these changes since no other group in American society will do it for them. Their dreams match Bloch's example of the hungry person who searches for food without considering the conditions that caused his or her hunger in the first place. Bloch makes it very clear that the fulfillment of *mere longing* dreams would not change anything in society at all. On the contrary, Bloch doubts even the fulfillment of many of these dreams, as an unchanged society does not offer conditions that would allow any fulfillment of such limited dreams. And indeed, the Peazants are so blinded by their own dreams that they do not realize that the North is not necessarily a place of new beginnings and power for everybody because it excludes Black people from the new bliss.

Their naïve belief about the North becomes clear in the stereoscopic viewer scene. Here the Unborn Child looks through a stereoscopic viewer and watches moving pictures of Northern cities. In those pictures the spectator can see hundreds and hundreds of people in the overcrowded Northern streets, busily hurrying from one important place to another, but among all those people, one cannot discover a single Black person. Nevertheless, the Unborn Child still naïvely concludes, "It was an age of beginnings, a time of promises. The newspaper said it was a time for everybody, the rich and the poor, the powerful and the powerless" (106). The stereoscopic viewer scene proves that the Peazants do not know the North at all, but have merely heard the success stories about it.

Of course, in the North the Peazants will not experience the specific form of openly displayed racism they have had to endure on the island, yet they will have to face a different form of racism, a more hidden, disguised one, but certainly no less in degree than the Southern form. However, right now, the Peazants still believe that simply the chance of living in real apartments and not in shacks anymore and of sending their children to real schools will guarantee them in every area of society the same degree of equality that most white Americans enjoy. Likewise, Viola truly believes that as soon as the women of her family know not to sit wide-legged on a chair and how to walk ladylike on high heels, they will no longer endure any discrimination as Black women.

Interestingly, the Peazants even get the chance to see the outcome of one limited *mere longing* dream since one of their family members, Yellow Mary, left the island many years ago with the same high hopes that all the Peazants are leaving with now. Like them, at the beginning of her journey Yellow Mary led a decent, married life and entertained high financial hopes and dreams of success. However, now she returns a little bit richer than they are, but as a prostitute.

Yet the Peazants are not using their chance of enlightening understanding. Since they are so blinded by their own dreams, they do not want to comprehend that Yellow Mary's dreams of financial and personal success failed because of the mainland's racist and sexist society that made sure Yellow Mary and her husband did not see the fulfillment of their dreams. For example, when Yellow Mary worked as a wet nurse for a family, she was treated without any respect or rights; in addition, her employer raped her repeatedly. Now, during her visit with her family, she tells Eula that this was the way she "got ruined" (126) and that that turned her into a prostitute. But the Peazants do not allow themselves to see any possible connections between Yellow Mary's failed dreams and their own high hopes because such a realization would carry a dangerous implication for the fulfillment of their own dreams. Instead, they choose to blame Yellow Mary herself for her failed life. Even when Yellow Mary tells them that "the raping of colored women is as common as the fish in the sea" (123), they still claim that it was all Yellow Mary's own mistake. They still believe that their own new life in the North will be completely different from Yellow Mary's and that, of course, their daughters will not face any similar problems.

Manthia Diawara explains that the Peazants still have to learn to "validate their identities as Americans of a distinctive culture."[115] Next to many other ideas,

---

[115] Diawara, "Black American Cinema," 15.

Diawara's statement implies also that the Peazants still have to learn to understand that many conditions which America claims to provide for everybody and which indeed apply to most white Americans will not apply to them as Black people. They still have to comprehend that they as African Americans have to take every societal condition and judge it from their specific African American situation, which is completely different from any other group's in American society.

Summarizing my ideas about Bloch's first dream category in connection to the Peazants, I claim that in general, everybody in the family except for Nana entertains his or her own private *mere longing* dream without any understanding of American society. As one result, nobody really has a dream or vision for the entire family together or for its future as an African American united group in the North.

As I showed earlier, one of *Daughters*' main concerns is African American unity and a common vision. Dash believes that such a common vision can be established only through the memory of Black history and culture. Emphasizing Dash's memory ideas in regard to a group vision, Jacquie Jones explains that in *Daughters*, "Dash authenticates the collective memory as essential and as necessarily [sic!]."[116] To illustrate her point about memory, Dash uses the image of the ancestors. According to her, the Peazants can succeed in any society, be it Southern or Northern, only if they begin to remember their ancestors' spirit and their determination to overcome any negative circumstances together as a united group. In regard to Bloch's theory, it can be claimed that the Peazants' ancestors were true Faustian characters because they lived with *enabling day dreams* from the second dream category; they had long-term visions for themselves as a group, seeing possible survival in a hostile and difficult

---

[116] Jacquie Jones, "The Black South in Contemporary Film," *African American Review* 27.1 (1993): 21.

environment only by being united. Simultaneously, they understood that white America was afraid of their Black unity and consequently tried hard to destroy any sense of it.

In *Daughters*, Nana reports that one of the many white attempts to rob Blacks of their unity was to not allow them to enjoy any form of family structure during slavery. Not only were they not allowed to marry, but couples were separated regardless of their feelings for each other. Slaves were regarded more as cattle than as humans as far as their personal emotions for each other were concerned: Men and women were forced to copulate for "breeding reasons," and children were taken away from their mothers sooner or later in order to be sold for profit.[117] However, even under such tremendously difficult circumstances, slaves fought for their sense of family. Nana remembers her ancestors during slavery time and tells about one of their attempts to keep family awareness:

> They didn't keep good records of our births, our deaths, or the selling of the slaves back then. A male child might be taken from his mother and sold at birth. Then, years later, this same person might have to mate with his own mother or sister, if they were brought back together again.... So it was important for the slave himself to keep the family ties. Just like the African Griot, who would hold these records in his head, the old souls in each family could recollect all the births, deaths, marriages and sales. (140/147).

These ancestors drew a lot of their spiritual strength needed for survival from myths about their unity. The most famous myth the Peazants generation lived with was the Ibo Landing myth. The story tells about the power and the pride of a group of Ibos who were captured in Africa and brought as slaves to the island where the Peazants live today. When these Ibo men, women, and children

---

[117] Toni Morrison's character Baby Suggs represents probably one of the emotionally most moving examples in American literature that illustrate this brutal practice during slavery. As I discussed in my *Beloved* chapter, in her case, in regard to the family-destroying practice during slavery, Baby Suggs reports that her eight children had six different fathers (24) and that all of her children except for one were sold or traded for lumber before they had their adult teeth (24). See Morrison, *Beloved.*

got off the slave ship, they took a good look around and saw why they had been brought to America and what was awaiting them. But instead of accepting their fate as slaves in a foreign country, they decided to turn around and walk back into the water: "They just kept walking, like the water was solid ground. And when they got to where the ship was, they didn't so much as give it a look. They just walked right past it, because they were going home" (142).

Because of the spiritual strength they drew from their myths, the earlier Peazant generations dared to have visions about their future as united Black people. Consequently, they were able to survive times that were much harder for Blacks than the situations the Peazants will face in the North. Nana recalls their past situation, "This was the worst place to have been born during slavery.... Our hands [were] scarred blue with the poisonous indigo dye that built up all those plantations from swampland..." (105). They were able to survive those deadly circumstances because, as the Unborn Child reports about them, "In this quiet place, years ago, my family knelt down and caught a glimpse of the eternal" (133). And this concept, which Dash calls "to catch a glimpse of the eternal," presents exactly Bloch's idea of *glimpses* and the *enabling day dream*: Their vision of their future survival as an African American group helped the early Peazants to not give up hope, thus avoiding a nihilistic mindset.[118] Nana reports that because of their enabling vision, they "*chose* to survive" (133)[119] even if they were thrown into circumstances that were life-destroying. Their decision of *choosing to survive* is a Blochian decision; Nana's ancestors survived bad

---

[118] In her interview with bell hooks, Julie Dash herself becomes something like a Faustian character when she talks about her own experience with the Ibo Landing myth and the reasons she included it in her movie. She explains that even today, people on every little island in this island chain claim this Ibo myth as their own and Ibo Landing as a geographic point of their own specific island. Therefore, Dash concludes, "It's because that message is so strong, so powerful, so sustaining to the tradition of resistance, by any means possible, that every Gullah community embraces this myth. So I learned that myth is very important in the struggle to maintain a sense of self and to move forward into the future." See Julie Dash, "Dialogue between bell hooks and Julie Dash," 30.

[119] Italics are mine—H. R.-H.

circumstances because they carried the concrete utopian hope that comes with *revolutionary forward dreaming.*

At the beginning of *Daughters*, Nana is the only family member left who knows about the ancestors' strength that came with their *revolutionary forward dreaming* and who has adopted this knowledge into her own life. Her ancestors' inspiring example of their determination to survive as Black people in a hostile white environment and to live with active hope helped Nana and her husband survive the difficult times during the Reconstruction period. Nana recalls one specific incident from that part of her life: When she was frustrated about the bad quality of the soil she and her husband had to plant in to make a living for themselves, she asked him, "Shad, how can we plant in this dust?" (158). He replied as a true offspring of people who *chose* to survive, "We plant each and every year, or we're finished" (158).

It is exactly this ancestral ability to find spiritual strength and vision, to "catch a glimpse of the eternal," that got lost with the later Peazant generations. Of course, they have kept the idea of inspiring their children to dream about better futures. Viola tells her friend Snead that the Peazants "spoil their children with dreams, wishes, magic" (136). Yet, as I have already argued, the problem is that whereas the earlier Peazants fed their children with dreams belonging to Bloch's second category, the current Peazants feed them only with dreams from the first category, reacting simply to their own filled emotions. But this is the crucial point where the current Peazants have to change. In Bloch's terminology, a change for them implies that the family members have to start the same *revolutionary forward dreaming* for their own self-empowerment like their ancestors lived with during their difficult times.

Right now, Nana is the only family member who realizes that the rest of the family does not share the ancestors' spirit but simply dreams in Bloch's *mere longing* category. At first, she comes across as the old woman who is upset about the departure of her entire family because it implies loneliness for her since she is staying behind on the island. At least, that is the interpretation of most of her relatives who watch Nana's depressed mood. Eli, for example, tells her, "Just because we're crossing over to the mainland, it doesn't mean that we don't love you. It doesn't mean that we're not going to miss you. And it doesn't mean that we're not going to come home and visit with you soon" (92). But Nana is upset because she recognizes that her family foolishly believes every story about the North without taking into consideration that as Black people they have to be very careful about the dreams society tells them to have. She observes that everybody is obsessed with the North without even asking what it really might mean for them: "North, they say. North is what they wake up whispering in their husbands' ears. That's the word that wets their lips in the nighttime" (86). She realizes that such a situation, with everybody merely dreaming for him- or herself without having any common dream or vision for the family as a whole, could happen only because most have lost their sense of unity.

This lost sense of unity can be observed during many incidents. For instance, when Yellow Mary returns home, most of the family members try to outdo each other in degrading her. Yellow Mary indeed stretches her family's tolerance to the extreme because she not only comes home as a quite well-to-do prostitute, but additionally brings with her another prostitute with whom she seems to have a lesbian relationship. Encountering Yellow Mary, all the other Peazant women suddenly seem very eager to show off their own spotless and righteous lives. They greet her with degrading and hateful remarks such as "All that yellow, wasted" (110), "…the heifer has returned" (110) and "The shameless hussy…" (111). When Yellow Mary offers cookies as a homecoming present, the reactions range from "I wouldn't eat them anyhow, if she touched them" (112) to "You never know where her hands could have been. I can just smell the heifer" (112). Nana and Eula are the only ones who greet Yellow Mary with love and express openly their joy about her return.

But then, Yellow Mary herself does not display a better attitude in regard to unity. Whenever she hears about some tradition her family is still practicing on the island, she laughs and calls individuals such as her cousin Eula "a real back-water Geechee girl" (120). Her attitude toward her family is very contradictory. On the one hand, she is glad to be back with them because of their excellent, traditional cooking skills; she tells her friend Trula, "Y'know, I sure hope they're fixing some gumbo. It's been a long time since I've had some good gumbo" (122). Yet, on the other hand, she looks down on their way of living and tells them repeatedly, "You live like savages back off in here" (121).

The Peazants' general disrespect for each other does not even stop with old members of the family. For instance, many regard Bilal, one of the last real Africans brought into American slavery, as an "old crazy man" (130) because he still keeps to African traditions and his Muslim religion. And Nana as well has to experience a great amount of disrespect from her own offspring. Haagar summarizes the family's general attitude toward Nana when she declares:

> I'm an educated person ... and I'm tired of Nana's old stories. Watching her make those root potions ... and that Hoodoo she talks about... washing up in the river with her clothes on, just like those old "Salt Water" folks used to do. My children ain't gonna be like those old Africans fresh off the boat. My God, I still remember them. (130)

Watching her family, Nana knows that they have lost any sense of unity. During one of the many family quarrels, she even breaks down and cries, "I can't understand how me and Peazant put you children here on earth to fight among yourselves.... You're the fruit of an ancient tree" (154). And Nana knows that without that sense of unity, her family will not survive in the North. As Yellow Mary "got ruined," they will get ruined, too, whatever this might imply for each of them individually. If they seriously intend to survive in a hostile white American society, they need to rediscover unity instead of falling more and more apart by disrespecting and degrading each other. Nana comprehends that a possible solution to their problem would involve the rediscovery of their ancestors' spirit since, again, the earlier Peazants survived the time of slavery and Reconstruction only because they perceived themselves as a united group who had a common vision about a possible future together.

Nana sees that most members of her family, in fact, think that they live with their ancestors' spirit because they observe several ancestral traditions. For example, some have a bottle tree in their yards, on which every single bottle stands for one former family member. Others have clippings from old newspapers on their walls, and some place a water glass underneath their bed during the night whenever they want one of the dead family members to appear in their night dreams. But for most family members, the ancestral connection stops there. This proves that they do not understand that ancestral inspiration is not necessarily connected to simply observing some old traditions. In contrast to Nana, who has a true spiritual connection to her ancestors, most of the other family members merely exercise these rituals as some leftover traditions without drawing any spiritual strength from them. Furthermore, they regard their ancestral myths as some old but otherwise not very important stories.

Here, too, they differ from Nana, who lives with the stories' inspirational powers. For example, most consider the Ibo Landing story simply a fairy tale. Bilal, for instance, claims that he knows the real truth about the Ibo myth and all other fairy tales. He tells Snead about the Ibo Landing, "Some say the Ibo flew back home to Africa. Some say they all joined hands and walked on top of the water. But, Mister, I was there. Those Ibo, men, women and children, a hundred or more, shackled in iron … when they went down in that water, they never came up. Ain't nobody can walk on water" (152). Bilal's attitude exemplifies most Peazant members' thinking, which prefers scientific truth over spiritual inspiration.

Other members, however, do not even observe those old traditions anymore. Some refuse to do so because they are highly embarrassed by such a culture. Haagar, for example, is glad that she is moving north, for she hopes that all that "tradition nonsense" will stop there. She tells Nana, "Where we're heading, Nana, there'll be no trees covered with glass jars in our yard. We'll have gardens of fresh flowers. Vegetables for the dinner table. Where we're heading, Nana, there'll be no need for an old woman's magic" (149).

Haagar makes it very clear that she herself will see to it that her daughters, who stand as symbols for the next generations in *Daughters*, will be completely separated from any ancestral knowledge. She declares in front of the entire family, "I want my daughters to grow up to be decent 'somebodies.' I don't even want my girls to have to *hear* about all that mess. I'll lock horns against anybody, anything that trys [sic!] to hold me back" (131).

Some other family members do not observe the family's ancestral traditions because they are already deep into Western religion. Viola, for instance, is torn between her respect for her grandmother and her Christian beliefs. On the one hand, she tells Haagar and another female family member who both make fun of Nana and her ancestral attitudes that they should stop their disrespectful behavior toward Nana. On the other hand, she herself tells Nana, "The Lord will carry us through, Nana. Trust in Jesus! Nana, we don't need any charms of dried roots and flowers" (150). Viola's limited view of her ancestors' spiritual powers makes her believe that Nana's concerns about the ancestors' guidance for the family's move up North are caused only by an old woman's desperate farewell pains.

Most of the family members' problems with the ancestral spirit result from their assumption that they are expected to take the meanings of these traditions and myths literally. Therefore, they display all their different attitudes such as rejecting their ancestors' spirit or not taking it seriously. Nana is the only one who understands that people need such traditions and myths for their spiritual power, or the *utopian surplus*, as Bloch would call it, and not for their literal meaning. She even tells Haagar, one of the biggest mockers of these traditions, that she considers her a fool for first taking everything so literally and then trying so hard to reject its literal meaning. When Haagar stands in front of the ancestors' bottle tree and screams, "As God's my witness … When I leave this place, never again will I live in your domain" (102), Nana watches her and tells her later:

> You are a natural fool, Haagar Peazant. Nobody ever said that the old souls were living inside those glass jars. The bottle tree reminds us who was here and who'se gone on. You study on the colors and shapes. You appreciate the bottle tree each day, as you appreciate your loved ones. (148)

Nana understands that her family has to learn the spiritual implication of those traditions. In addition, Nana sees that if her family does not learn ancestral spirituality while still on their ancestors' home island, they will simply never discover any spiritual strength because in the outside white world, they will be too busy fighting daily encounters of sexist and racist oppression. Therefore, she decides to fight for them.

A text that can be called a Blochian concrete utopia cannot only analyze a situation, but it needs to show its protagonists *en route* to their *ultimate, true human identity* if it intends to inspire its readers. *Daughters* succeeds in this regard. In the movie, the personal growth of the Peazants happens because of Nana, the Faustian representative in *Daughters*. She becomes the catalyst for a spiritual reawakening for the family. Nana is able to function as such a catalyst because, as I have shown, she has kept the ancestors' true spirit. Therefore, she can also declare about herself, "I was the tie between then and now. Between the past and the story that was to come" (107). Even other elders in the family testify to Nana's function as the ancestral tie. Daddy Mac, for example, explains the connection between the ancestors and Nana: "We Peazants come from a long line of creation and hope, begun by those first-captured Africans. And Nana, Nana carried them with her" (147).

Nana sees her task now in teaching her family the spirit of the ancestors who knew how to dream as in Bloch's second dream category. As one part of her attempt, she addresses individual members with sentences like "Respect your elders! Respect your family! Respect your ancestors" (94). For example, when she tries to help her grandson Eli with his specific problem, she tells him, "Those in the grave, like those who are across the sea, they're with us. They're all the same. The ancestors and the womb are one. Call on your ancestors, Eli. Let them guide you. You need their strength, Eli" (95). When Eli responds that when he was young, he indeed believed in the powers of his ancestors, but now, as a grown man, he has seen too much misery done to Black people and consequently cannot trust her "old people talk" anymore, she nevertheless urges him:

> Do you believe that hundreds and hundreds of Africans brought here on this side would forget everything they once knew? We don't know where the recollections come from. Sometimes we dream them. But we carry these memories inside of us.... I'm trying to teach you how to touch your own spirit. I'm fighting for my life, Eli, and I'm fighting for yours.... I'm trying to give you something to take North with you, along with all your big dreams.... Call on those old Africans.... Let them feed your head with wisdom that ain't from this day and time. Because when you leave this island, Eli Peazant, you ain't going to no land of milk and honey. (96-97)

Here in her speech it becomes very clear what Nana implies with her urge to "respect your elders": Eli needs to allow his thoughts and dreams to be influenced by his ancestors' attitudes if he wants to discover his own true self or, as Bloch would call it, his *ultimate true human identity*.

Since part of the ancestors' spirit deals with their vision of themselves as a united group, Nana decides that the healing process has to start with the rediscovery of unity among the individual family members. In this regard, Nana receives help from one of her granddaughters, Eula, who has been the one family member who has come closest to the idea of preserving the ancestors' and Nana's spirit. Other family members even see this continuation of Nana's spirit in Eula because they make fun of her and decide to give Nana's old Hoodoo tools to Eula since she is "as crazy as Nana" (128).

Hence, it is possible that after some time Eula becomes a Faustian representative, too, thus acting as an agent for the healing process. She helps the other Peazants during their journey to unity in one particular case, the community's move toward tolerance and love of Yellow Mary. The ultimate change in her family's attitude toward Yellow Mary happens when Eula observes so much hatred among the Peazant women that she breaks down and cries:

> As far as this place is concerned, we never enjoyed our womanhood.... Deep inside, we believed that they ruined our mothers, and their mothers before them. And we live our lives always expecting the worst because we feel we don't deserve any better.... You think you can cross over to the mainland and run away from it? You're going to be sorry, sorry if you don't change your way of thinking before you leave this place.... If you love yourselves, then love Yellow Mary, because she's part of you.... We carry too many scars from the past. Our past owns us.... Let's live our lives without living in the fold of old wounds. (156-157)

In this scene, Eula proves that she fully understands the Peazants' dilemma with the past and the present. Using the example of the Black woman's situation in American history, Eula attempts to show her family that they have tried for too long to ignore the true African American past and have somewhat blinded themselves with some other made-up ideas. Therefore, she tells them about their dilemma: "Deep inside we believe that even God can't heal the wounds of our past or protect us from the world that put shackles on our feet" (156).

Eula's true Blochian side becomes obvious when she not only understands this dilemma but knows that a possible solution can lie only in personal agency. She understands that they all have to face reality and work as a community instead of believing that society will bring them individual happiness. Her call to agency is clearly expressed in her urging, "If you love yourself, then love Yellow Mary, because she is part of you. Just like we are part of our mothers. A lot of us are going through things we feel we can't handle all alone" (157).

Because of Eula's urging, most members finally realize how far their hatred and disrespect have already carried them. Even if they cannot bring themselves to embrace Yellow Mary as Nana and Eula do, they at least feel ashamed of their attitudes and mumble something like apologies. In addition, they now understand Eula's insistence on seeing how the past really happened rather than how most of them have tried to invent it by simply deleting certain negative memories and events. The specific example of the Black woman's situation in American history helps the Peazants to now understand Eula's insistence that "we've got to change our way of thinking" (157). Now they finally realize that they have to see themselves as a particular group with a specific history. Their new understanding of American history helps them situate themselves correctly in American society.

Since they now comprehend that as African Americans they have to judge and consider each everyday life situation from a different perspective than white Americans do, they realize at last that their dreams about the North have to change and be adjusted. Here, too, their ancestors' spirit serves them as role model. For example, in regard to their women, the Peazants' ancestors could not afford to dream about womanhood the same way white women could dream about their virtues and their true womanhood.[120] Of course, they could be angry and frustrated about the Black woman's situation and hope that in the future, justice might be served to her, but they knew they could not afford to blame the victim because it would have destroyed their unity as Black people. If they had started to blame the victim, they first would have had to blame the woman who got ruined, and then the man who did not protect her, and then they would have been busy blaming each other for their failures. The same way their ancestors could not merely participate in the great American dream but rather had to find dreams that corresponded to their own particular situation first as slaves and then as free, but

[120] For a detailed analysis of key ideas such as piety, purity, submissiveness, and domesticity connected to the nineteenth century American philosophy of true womanhood, see Barbara Welter, "The Cult of True Womanhood: 1820-1860," *American Quarterly* 18 (1966): 151-174.

still oppressed, people, the Peazants must reevaluate their situation and rethink their dreams about success in the North.

As far as the family's healing is concerned, Eli's healing process serves as a good example of a particular personal transformation. His conversion occurs when he secretly listens to Eula telling the Ibo Landing story to her unborn child. Here Eula emphasizes to her child, who symbolizes the next generations, the importance of the ancestors' spirit for all following generations in regard to overcoming obstacles. Watching his wife's close connection to her ancestors and their wisdom, Eli suddenly understands his grandmother's urge to respect the ancestors. He sees that Nana's message to him, too, is that their ancestors survived and empowered themselves only because they did not blame each other for their miseries. They saw that although most of their negative circumstances had been caused by white society, they still could not afford to remain in a state of self-pity and lamentation. Instead, they chose unity over self-pity and looked toward the future. With this new understanding of his ancestors, Eli is finally able to allow their spirit to guide his thoughts and dreams. As a result, he can now accept Eula's child as his, too, and can begin to dream together with his wife about the future.

Even if most people in the family have now realized the importance of the ancestors' spirit and of unity among them, Nana still wants to teach them that they should not only remember those concepts in times of crisis but should live with them permanently, especially during their new lives in the North. To emphasize her ideas, Nana chooses her formal blessing ceremony and prepares a tool for the ceremony, a "charm bag." Into this bag, which looks like a hand, she places several items that belonged to some of her former family members. For example, she includes a lock of her mother's hair, which her mother gave Nana when she was sold away from her children during slavery. Nana places a lock of her own hair into the charm bag, too, for she hopes that these personal ancestral items will convince her children that "there must be a bond, a connection, between those that go up North, and those who [sic!] across the sea" (157).

In the evening when she gives her maternal blessing to everyone who will depart the next day, she places her charm bag on Viola's Bible. Then she asks every person who finally understands the importance of the ancestors' spirit for his or her own life to greet the bag and the Bible with a kiss. Resembling a Christian communion celebration, this scene becomes the central scene for the movie, for it is here that Nana can celebrate her victory in her fight for her family. Sara Clarke Kaplan emphasizes that the merging of the symbols of both religions here demonstrates that "through the open-ended engagement with a shared history of subjugation and opposition, formerly enslaved people and their descendants produce and sustain situated practices and places of diasporicity capable of intervening in contemporary material and discursive structures of racism."[121]

Concerning their community celebration and the ancestral "glimpses of the eternal," at this point everybody except for Haagar finally decides that he or she wants to take the ancestors' wisdom to the new world, the North. Even Mr. Snead, the photographer, who is not family, decides that he wants to be part of the Peazants' ancestral knowledge and guidance. His participation as a non-Peazant symbolizes the idea that the concept of ancestral inspiration is not merely an isolated family affair but involves the entire African American community. Noting the changes in Snead's character during the course of the movie, Toni Cade Bambara says about him, "Initially bemused, curious about the backwoods folk Viola regards as heathens, he becomes the anthropologist who learns from 'his photographic subjects.' After interviewing people on the island, Snead discovers a more profound sense of his own self."[122] In the end, he, too, becomes a Blochian character whose search for *his ultimate true human identity* has been successful.

---

[121] Sara Clarke Kaplan, "Souls at the Crossroads, Africans on the Water: The Politics of Diasporic Melancholia," *Callaloo* 30.2 (2007): 512.

[122] Bambara, "Reading the Signs," 133.

During Nana's ceremony, Viola represents one of the most struggling and resisting characters. At first, she not only refuses to participate in Nana's ceremony but in addition urges in great agony for everybody else to realize that the ceremony stands for evil according to her Christian definition. She shouts at every participating family member, "It's not right! We're supposed to die and go to heaven! What you're doing is wrong!" (161). However, even Viola comes to understand that the Peazants' ability to envision another future and to empower themselves is not related at all to any form of Hoodoo magic and does not endanger her Christian values.

For Viola, Julie Dash offers a unique solution during her healing process toward the *ultimate, true human identity*. Because Viola suffers from the problem of considering her own culture inferior to the white one, Dash does not make her renounce her newfound religion, but offers the idea of a completely new culture merging out of two old ones. Dash uses the idea that the term "African American" implies two different aspects that meet and create a completely new, unique culture. Here in *Daughters*, the merging of the two different parts is expressed in Nana's ceremony with the charm bag, the symbol for the African part, and Viola's Bible, the symbol for the Western tradition. Thus, even someone like Viola gets the chance to experience an ancestral spiritual regeneration since she now comprehends that the African American culture does not ask for an either/or decision but results from merging. She is finally able to understand that accepting her African side does not imply any denouncement of her Christian beliefs. On the contrary, the merging of the Bible and the bag allows her to understand her self as a unique product of both the African and the Western traditions.

In the end, the members of the Peazant family successfully complete their spiritual journeys that Bloch's concrete utopian theory requires from Faustian representatives. Since they have rediscovered their ancestors' ability to envision a different future for themselves as an African American group, thus exercising self-empowerment, they will leave the island with the ability to stand united as a group. With their new knowledge and ability they will be able to face the sexist and racist problems in the North.

I argued that the Peazants initially dream in Bloch's *mere longing* category but have to learn to dream in the *revolutionary forward dreaming* category. In the end, several members indeed have learned to dream in Bloch's second category, implying that they have changed their dreams from immediate, egocentric desires to long-term concerns about the larger society and with real changes regarding not only individuals but the group as a whole.

Exemplifying these already changed members' move into the second dream category, Eli's case serves as a good example of such a transformation. As I showed earlier, Eli's *mere longing* dream was to avenge his male pride without considering what his dream might imply for his life and for his family. After his spiritual transformation, he transfers his dreams from the first to the second category. The Unborn Child testifies to this transfer when she reports that in the end he does not move north, but stays behind on the island and begins to work in the anti-lynching campaign. Instead of running blindly into his own lynching by insisting on avenging his male pride, he now works on changing society to the point where lynching becomes a legally punishable crime. The changed Eli allows hope that others will follow and will change their dreams, thus perhaps working on making the rape of Black women a legally punishable crime, for example.

As Eli has learned *revolutionary forward dreaming*, the other members, too, have discovered a new wisdom about themselves and their personal agency. In the end of *Daughters*, Nana testifies to her family's new wisdom when she uses exactly the same words the Unborn Child used about the Peazants' ancestors and which contain the Blochian program; in the end, Nana observes about her family, "In this quiet place, simple folk knelt down and caught a glimpse of the eternal" (163). Seeing that she succeeded in her task of helping her family *en route*, Nana is finally able to rejoice during their departure: "Morning would begin a new life for my children and me. They would carry my spirit. I would remain here, with the old souls!" (163).

As I mentioned in my introduction, after the success of her film, Julie Dash actually published a novel with the same title, *Daughters of the Dust.*[123] In her book, Dash follows the Peazants to the North to see whether they do indeed succeed in their quest for dream fulfillments. For my thesis of the Blochian concrete utopian empowerment, Dash's novel is intriguing because one can actually observe that the newly discovered self-empowerment, caused by the "glimpses of the eternal," the *utopian surplus*, enabled several Peazants—the ones who stayed behind on the island, Eula, Eli, and the Unborn Child—to keep working on their particular societal circumstances. In the book, Amelia, one of Haagar's granddaughters, who was born in the North, returns as an anthropology student to her family on Dawtah Island. Like Snead, the photographer, at first she considers the island Peazants as objects to be studied, but she soon realizes that they have so much more to offer to her.

At the beginning of this chapter, I stated that Julie Dash intended her film *Daughters of the Dust* for the African American community at the end of the twentieth century. She hoped that its members would understand that their strength lies in each other and in their unity. Attempting to achieve such an understanding, Dash used *Daughters* to make them aware of their distinctive history and culture. Regarding this specific accomplishment of *Daughters*, Greg Tate claims in his discussion of the movie that *Daughters* indeed succeeds in this point. Analyzing the situation of African Americans in the 1990s, Tate explains, "We remain in a middle passage, living out an identity that is neither African nor American, though we crave for both shores to claim us. It is *Daughters*'

---

[123] Julie Dash, *Daughters of the Dust* (New York: Dutton, 1997).

achievement to represent this double alienation as an issue for the community as a whole."[124]

And Dash not only represents this double alienation; she also offers healing. If, then, African American viewers of *Daughters* compare their own situations with the Peazants' healing process and receive inspiration for their own personal agency in their own respective realities, *Daughters* succeeds in providing the empowerment through fictitious visions that Bloch asks from concrete utopias.

---

[124] Greg Tate, "A Word," *Daughters of the Dust. The Making of an African American Woman's Film*, by Julie Dash (New York: The New Press, 1992) 71.

Chapter 5

Healing Communities

Ernst Bloch and Contemporary African American Women Writers

In Toni Cade Bambara's *The Salt Eaters*, the protagonist, Velma Henry, after trying to commit suicide, is asked by Minnie Ransom, her spiritual healer, "Are you sure, sweetheart, that you want to be well?"[125] Minnie asks the question because she realizes that Velma's body can heal only when Velma herself first decides that she wants to heal spiritually, too. Minnie Ransom's question about self-activated, chosen healing points to Bloch's idea of self-empowerment. Velma's mental breakdown resulted from spiritual burnout and disappointment about her civil-rights community in which the women always end up doing the tedious, dirty, time- and energy-consuming work while the men show up in "shiny sunglasses and silk-and-steel suits"[126] to give well-polished, boring speeches in public and lament the betrayal of the women in private. To change those

---

[125] Toni Cade Bambara, *The Salt Eaters* (New York: Vintage Books, 1980) 3.

[126] Bambara, *The Salt Eaters*, 35.

circumstances would imply that Velma herself, as one of the exploited women, also has to get involved together with all the other women. However, she has just demonstrated that she refuses to be part of any agenda anymore. Consequently, before anything else, Velma's attitude has to change, and, according to Bloch, Velma herself is the only one who can do this. The process of becoming aware of her own agency will lead to her self-empowerment. Only after her self-empowerment will she be able to work on the community's changes. Like all the other characters I discussed in my previous chapters, Velma, too, becomes a Faustian representative because eventually she does decide for self-empowerment, which, in turn, will help her to become an active member of her community again.

Velma's self-activated healing process carries the utopian hope impulse that is supposed to inspire the reader toward his or her own agency. As I argued in my introduction, I observe Blochian concrete utopian hope in many texts by contemporary African American women writers since the late 1970s, such as Alice Walker, Toni Morrison, Gloria Naylor, Paule Marshall, Maya Angelou, Gayl Jones, Toni Cade Bambara, Sherley Anne Williams, Ntozake Shange, Bebe More Campbell, and Terry McMillan, just to name the major authors.

These writers differ significantly from their predecessors because they do not limit their fiction to descriptions of reality and mere criticism of negative societal circumstances, but they enter the realm of "prophesy" by including visions of healed Black women. Unlike the preceding writers such as Nella Larsen, Jessie Fauset, Ann Petry, and Dorothy West, who depicted spiritually broken Black women who were unable to liberate themselves from oppression, the writers of the following period—which include several generations by now—provide visions of Black women who, with the help of some form of community, have found the necessary self-esteem and self-empowerment to overcome racist, sexist, and economic oppression. Speaking of Morrison, for example, Barbara

Christian argues that in her novels, Morrison "makes an attempt … to figure out the possibilities of healing and community for her women characters."[127]

Whereas Barbara Christian looks at one author in particular, other critics emphasize the healing motif in the texts of the Black contemporary women writers in general. Joanne V. Gabbin, for example, claims that because of these writers, a transformation has happened in African American literature because for the first time, African American women have been "cleansing, healing and empowering the images of themselves."[128] Susan Willis sees the unifying contribution of these texts in the writers' capacity to imagine "the future in the present, [a] future born out of the context of oppression. It produces utopia out of the transformation of the most basic features of daily life."[129] Willis's idea connects the texts to Bloch's *anticipatory illumination* of the *not-yet*, or, in other Blochian terms, they display the capacity for *revolutionary dreaming ahead.*

Bloch argues that the *anticipatory illumination* of the *not-yet* can be expressed only in fragments because the longing for the *ultimate true human identity* differs for everybody in regard to the historical, social, and cultural context. His premise of the specific fragmental hope applies to the texts of the discussed authors, too. Sometimes one might hear scholarly voices that argue that these discussed contemporary African American women writers constitute a somewhat monolithic group in regard to their experiences of race and gender oppression in American society; however, it is important to note that all their texts differ greatly from each other precisely because such a monolithic, general Black women's experience does not exist in African American reality. As I have shown

---

[127] Barbara Christian, "Trajectories of Self-Definition: Placing Contemporary Afro-American Women's Fiction," *Black Feminist Criticism* (New York: Pergamon Press, 1985) 180.

[128] Joanne V. Gabbin, "A Laying On of Hands: Black Women Writers Exploring the Roots of Their Folk and Cultural Tradition," *Wild Women in the Whirlwind. Afra-American Culture and the Contemporary Literary Renaissance*, eds. Joanne M. Braxton and Andree Nicola McLaughlin (New Brunswick: Rutgers University Press, 1990) 247.

[129] Susan Willis, *Specifying. Black Women Writing the American Experience* (Madison: University of Wisconsin Press, 1987) 159.

in my introduction, many African American scholars such as Mae Henderson or Cheryl Wall have cautioned us against such a simplistic and even dangerous discourse. These texts do not depict a general Black community, but rather deal with very diverse, specific circumstances. Barbara Christian points out that the texts refuse "all-encompassing definitions of the black community or the black man or the black woman and [emphasize] the concept of difference that [is] so central to the literature and criticism of the seventies and eighties."[130] In every novel, one can observe another specific fragment that deals with the Blochian striving toward the *ultimate true human identity*.

Bambara's *The Salt Eaters*, for example, asks Black social activists to realize that many more issues than merely the obvious race-related civil rights questions should be part of their current political agenda because "drugs, prisons, alcohol, the schools, rape, battered women, abused children [and] the nuclear power issue"[131] belong together. To illustrate her point, Bambara has two African American social activists, Jan and Ruby, discuss this problem. When Ruby complains, "All this doomsday mushroom-cloud end-of-planet numbah is past my brain. Just give me the good ole-fashioned honky-nigger shit. I think all this ecology stuff is a diversion," Jan replies:

> They're connected. Whose community do you think they ship radioactive waste through, or dig up waste burial grounds near? Who do you think they hire for the dangerous dirty work at those plants? What parts of the world do they test-blast in? And all them illegal uranium mines dug up on Navajo turf—the crops dying, the sheep dying, the horses, water, cancer, Ruby, cancer. And the plant on the Harlem river and—Ruby, don't get stupid on me.[132]

---

[130] Barbara Christian, "Literature since 1970," *African-American Literature. The Norton Anthology*, eds. Henry Louis Gates, Jr. and Nellie Y. McKay (New York: W.W. Norton, 1997) 2016.

[131] Bambara, *The Salt Eaters*, 198.

[132] Bambara, *The Salt Eaters*, 242.

Because of visionary fiction like this, it has been said of Toni Cade Bambara that she "made revolution irresistible," as Toni Morrison recalls.[133]

Other writers dedicate their fragmental search for the *ultimate true human identity* to the connection between the slavery past and subsequent generations. Morrison's *Beloved* and *Jazz* as well as Gayl Jones's *Corregidora* deal with the devastating psychological effects that slavery can still have on following generations. In Jones's novel, sexuality becomes the locus of identity. *Corregidora's* protagonist Ursa and her mother are not able to develop healthy relationships with men because their foremothers were the products of abuse and rape and, in addition, were forced into prostitution during slavery times. Amy Gottfried explains about Ursa and her mother that although they themselves "have never been slaves, [slavery's] ideology of black sexuality permeates their relationship[s]."[134] This is possible because their foremothers had decided to tell the next generations in detail about the abuse in order to prevent their experiences of sexual exploitation from being forgotten. Cheryl Wall points out that the pain and despair *Corregidora* conveys make it "a difficult book to read."[135] She observes that "the novel is unsparing in its depiction of the rawness of the hate that develops instead of love."[136] The depiction of this "rawness of hate" was indeed intentional of Ursa's foremothers, for they wanted every following female generation to inherit their own hatred of men. Ursa explains the idea of maternal oral tradition passed on to the next daughter:

---

[133] Toni Morrison, Preface, *Deep Sighting and Rescue Missions. Fictions, Essays, and Conversations*, Toni Cade Bambara (New York: Pantheon Books, 1996) xi.

[134] Amy Gottfried, "Angry Arts: Silence, Speech, and Song in Gayl Jones's *Corregidora*," *African American Review* 28.4 (1994): 565.

[135] Cheryl Wall, *Worrying the Line. Black Women Writers, Lineage, and Literary Tradition* (Chapel Hill and London: The University of North Carolina Press, 2005) 118.

[136] Wall, *Worrying the Line*, 117.

> My great-grandmother told my grandmother the part she lived through that my grandmother didn't live through and my grandmother told my mama what they both lived through and my mama told me what they all lived through and we were suppose [sic!] to pass it down like that from generation to generation so we'd never forget.[137]

By passing on this hatred, Ursa's foremothers had hoped to ensure that every following daughter would identify with motherhood only, but not with a possible partnership or any form of sexual pleasure. Since Ursa and her mother have grown up with this attitude implanted in their brains, they indeed display a hostile attitude toward sexuality in their relationships. Therefore, their partnerships start out as somewhat normal, but end up in abuse and domestic violence. Ursa's mother is beaten by her husband until her face is swollen and discolored, and Ursa is pushed down a flight of stairs by her own husband, which kills her fetus and requires her to have a hysterectomy.

Morrison's *Jazz*, too, focuses on the spiritual effects slavery still has on following generations. However, whereas *Beloved*'s people and *Corregidora*'s women suffer from too much connectedness to their past, in *Jazz*, the characters suffer from a disconnectedness from each other. Philip Page explains that the characters in *Jazz* "have trouble developing fulfilled selves because they lack adequate relationships with one or more others, such as parents, spouse, family, neighborhood, community, and/or society."[138] This lack of adequate relationships is still a product of slavery because to prevent any unity among Black people, slave holders deliberately created disconnectedness in the Black family. Unfortunately, subsequent generations have not had the chance to work consciously through this problem. As a result, the disconnectedness still haunts

---

[137] Gayl Jones, *Corregidora* (Boston: Beacon Press, 1975) 9.

[138] Philip Page, "Traces of Derrida in Toni Morrison's *Jazz*," *African American Review* 29.1 (1995): 55. For a general discussion on community in African American literature, see also Philip Page's detailed analysis: Philip Page, *Reclaiming Community in Contemporary African American Fiction* (Jackson: University Press of Mississippi, 1999).

later generations and influences their own decisions about personal relationships. In *Jazz*, Morrison offers this disconnectedness with her two protagonists, Joe and Violet, whom she places into the historical period of the Great Migration. Joe, for example, suffers from the fact that he is not able to verify his parents' existence: A father never really existed, and his mother, a wild woman who supposedly lives in the woods, abandoned him at birth. Violet's fate does not look much better because her father took off to the North to make his fortune, leaving his wife and five small children behind in tremendous poverty, which eventually caused her mother to commit suicide. As a result of her traumatic childhood experiences, Violet refuses to have children of her own, but sleeps with dolls in her arms. Because Joe and Violet have never experienced lasting and loving relationships, their own marriage has lost any notion of a fulfilled relationship. Hoping that a geographic relocation will change that, they become part of the Great Migration and move north. However, their move does not improve anything. On the contrary, now not only are they "barely speaking to each other, let alone laughing together or acting like the ground [is] a dance-hall floor,"[139] but Joe begins an affair with a teenage girl whom he murders without any obvious reason after a short time together.

Sherley Anne Williams's *Dessa Rose* uses the historical period of slavery, too, but unlike *Beloved, Jazz*, and *Corregidora*, which are more interested in depicting the spiritual damage of slavery on subsequent generations, *Dessa Rose* uses slavery to test the possibilities for an equal society between Black and white people. In her novel, Williams examines the degree to which people have to change their personalities in order to truly respect each other as equals. For her testing ground, she employs Ruth, a white woman who hides runaway slaves on her farm where she in general perceives herself as a generous woman. Not only does she protect the Black people from being caught again, but in addition, she has an affair with one of the slaves, and she nurses one of the slave babies when

[139] Toni Morrison, *Jazz* (New York: Alfred A. Knopf, 1992) 37.

the baby's mother is physically not able to do so. However, Ruth lives in a fantasy world, believing that her actions cause the Black people around her to love her. She still has to learn that equality does not happen because of some isolated actions but because of total respect for the other person, a respect that allows the other person to choose friendship freely for him- or herself without being made to do so.

Taking place in a historical period long after slavery, but nevertheless addressing the problem of disconnectedness, Paule Marshall's *Praisesong for the Widow* could also be called *Daughters of the Dust, Part II* because Marshall places her protagonist, Avey Johnson, into prosperous circumstances in the North, something the Peazants still dream about. Indeed, like a possible Peazant offspring with U.S. roots in South Carolina, Avey's husband "works two jobs, goes to night school, and, with extraordinary determination, moves himself and the family into the middle class [and] as the final symbol of their success ... [they] move to the suburbs, to a destination that is the polar opposite of rural South Carolina: North White Plains,"[140] as Cheryl Wall depicts it. But as *Daughters*' great-grandmother, Nana, always has feared for her family, Avey has indeed lost any connection to her ancestors and her origin. Abena Busia explains that the novel "takes us through a private history of material acquisition and cultural dispossession, which becomes a metaphor for the history of the group, the history of the African in the New World."[141] As a result, Avey ends in a nearly life-destroying spiritual crisis that is exemplified in her inability to answer the questions, "And what you is? What your nation?"[142]

Other writers choose for their fragmental search a completely different focus: the Black woman's sexual and mental abuse in the Black community itself.

---

[140] Wall, *Worrying the Line*, 183.

[141] Abena P.A. Busia, "What Is Your Nation?: Reconnecting Africa and Her Diaspora through Paule Marshall's *Praisesong for the Widow*," *Changing Our Own Words*, ed. Cheryl Wall (New Brunswick and London: Rutgers University Press, 1989) 197.

[142] Paule Marshall, *Praisesong for the Widow* (New York: Penguin Books, 1983) 167.

Alice Walker's *The Color Purple* would present an example for such a focus. In Ntozake Shange's *for colored girls who have considered suicide / when the rainbow is enuf*, too, Black women are not raped and abused by strangers but by the Black men with whom they have relationships. In Gloria Naylor's *The Women of Brewster Place*, women are fooled into pregnancies they never wanted but are made to abort the babies they did want. They are raped by neighborhood gangs and physically and mentally abused by the men to whom they offered their love. Terry McMillan, too, focuses on the withered lives of Black women due to the mainly mental abuse by their own men in *Waiting to Exhale* and *Disappearing Acts*.

In comparison to all previously mentioned texts, Alice Walker's *Possessing the Secret of Joy* moves its fragmental search for the *ultimate true human identity* into a completely different terrain. Instead of making the African American woman her topic, Walker concentrates on the story of an African woman, Tashi. With Tashi's story, Walker shows that sexual abuse can imply many more additional aspects, in this case genital mutilation. In *Possessing*, Walker depicts the life-destroying effects this particular form of sexual oppression has for the victim. For example, as one result of her genital mutilation, Tashi is not able to be a sexual partner to Adam, her husband. Every attempt at intercourse with him turns into a disaster. In addition, Tashi has to sacrifice her dreams about happy, normal motherhood. The birth of Benny, her son, becomes a horrible experience for her. Because of the difficult birth, Benny is permanently retarded. Out of fear of repeating her experiences again, Tashi aborts her second pregnancy, the daughter she had always wished for.

All these texts deal with different specific historical, social, and cultural aspects of Black reality; nevertheless, they all share a common basis in regard to Bloch's theory. They all start their protagonists in negative circumstances, but then they gradually provide their protagonists with the chance to grow, to survive, and finally to celebrate. The critic Chinosole's statement about Audre Lorde's texts that move "history beyond nightmare into structures for the future"[143] applies to all the texts under discussion. The title of Maya Angelou's first autobiography, *I Know Why the Caged Bird Sings*, embodies the whole idea of this shared basis of surviving and celebrating. The protagonists' transformational process contains the concrete *utopian impulse* that will transfer its inspiration to the reader.

However, to call the protagonists' healing process a Blochian concrete utopian transformation, the protagonist has to become consciously aware of his or her own responsibility for changes. He or she has to choose his or her transformation and has to become actively involved in it. Minnie Ransom's question in *The Salt Eaters*, "Are you sure, sweetheart, that you want to be well?"[144] exemplifies the Blochian concept of the protagonist's conscious choice of personal agency. Concerning this necessity of personal choice, Toni Morrison even picks up Maya Angelou's bird image in her Nobel Prize lecture in which she, referring to an old parable, lets the parable's old woman state that "the bird is in your hands," implying that "if it is dead, you have either found it that way or you have killed it. If it is alive, you can still kill it. Whether it is to stay alive, it is your decision. Whatever the case, it is your responsibility."[145] Indeed, realizing that the "bird is in [one's] hand," in every discussed text, the protagonist fulfills this Blochian requirement of choosing transformation.

In addition to the conscious choice, one can observe in every single case that the healing process does not happen because of some sudden miracle or some fast remedies, but rather as the result of a long and often painful process. During

---

[143] Chinosole, "Audre Lorde and Matrilineal Diaspora: Moving History beyond Nightmare into Structures for the Future," *Wild Women in the Whirlwind*, eds. Joanne M. Braxton and Andree Nicola McLaughlin (New Brunswick: Rutgers University Press, 1990) 379.

[144] Bambara, *The Salt Eaters*, 3.

[145] Toni Morrison, "The Bird Is in Your Hands," *Nobel Lectures from the Literature Laureates 1986 to 2006*, ed. The Nobel Foundation (New York and London: The Free Press, 2007) 183.

their transformation, the protagonists go through many stages of self-doubt and of questioning facts that they had previously believed to be indisputable knowledge. In their search for understanding and healing, they are often guided by other people, mostly women, who serve as catalysts for the protagonists' healing process.

I have already described the healing process for Sethe in *Beloved*, who is on her way to put her painful past into the correct perspective in order to gain a meaningful future. The same healing process can be observed with Celie in *The Color Purple*, who first learns to love and respect herself and then to stand up for her own rights and demand respect from all the people who have mistreated her physically and mentally. This also applies to the people in *Bailey's Café* whom Naylor sends on spiritual journeys to let them experience and finally gain the possibility of healing. And the Peazant family members in *Daughters of the Dust* begin to spiritually heal because they succeed in their search for ancestral power and guidance.

In Marshall's *Praisesong*, Avey Johnson suffers from the same ancestral problems the Peazants did; Barbara Christian explains that she "must discard her American value of obsessive materialism, must return to her source, must remember the ancient wisdom of African culture—that the body and soul are one, that harmony cannot be achieved unless there is a reciprocal relationship between the individual and the community."[146] Her transformation starts when she leaves the cruise ship while on a trip in the Caribbean and tries to go home to New York City but gets stuck on a little ferry boat where she encounters the spiritual powers of some islander women. On the boat, she gets physically sick, but Rosalie Parvay, a native from one of the islands, immediately understands Avey's physical illness to be the result of some spiritual misery. Until this point, Avey has not been aware of the true cause for her spiritual restlessness. As Cheryl Wall observes, after her attempted flight from the cruise ship, Avey is haunted like a

---

[146] Christian, "Trajectories of Self-Definition," 181.

slave during an escape, yet "unlike the fugitive slave, she cannot explain what she is escaping from."[147] Because of Rosalie, who now becomes her catalyst, Avey is able to start her spiritual search for her true ancestral essence.

Her healing process climaxes when she participates in the "Big Drum" festival on Carriacou. Watching others perform the dance for the "old People" makes her realize that "it [is] the essence of something rather than the thing itself."[148] Participating in the Ring Shout concludes her spiritual healing. Because she allows herself to be part of the ceremony, she experiences that the "elderly Shouters in the person of the out-islanders had reached out their arms like one great arm and drawn her into their midst."[149] She expresses her completed healing in her ability to remember the name that was given to her by her ancestors: Avatara.

In Morrison's *Jazz*, Violet's transformation begins with her visits with Alice Manfred, the aunt of the teenage girl Violet's husband, Joe, had murdered. Initially, Violet visits Alice Manfred only with the intention of seeing a picture and getting an impression of her husband's dead girlfriend to deepen her own inferiority complex as a woman and to bathe in her self-pity about nobody loving someone like her. However, during these visits, Alice helps Violet start the healing process because of her special, aggressive way in dealing with Violet; Morrison depicts her as "impolite. Sudden. Frugal. No apology or courtesy seemed required or necessary between them."[150] In this manner, she does not allow Violet to drown in her own self-pity, but forces her to face reality. Although Violet originally decided not to talk to anyone anymore for the rest of her life, she regains her voice during her visits with Alice Manfred.

---

[147] Wall, *Worrying the Line*, 195.

[148] Marshall, *Praisesong for the Widow*, 240.

[149] Marshall, *Praisesong for the Widow*, 248.

[150] Morrison, *Jazz*, 83.

During their talks, one can observe that Alice indeed becomes the necessary catalyst for Violet's transformation because, as Lucilla Fultz explains, "Conversations with Violet reveal Alice's own desire ... to kill her husband's lover and lead to her understanding of Violet' mutilation of Dorca's [Joe's dead girl-friend] corpse."[151] However, with Alice, Violet watches a woman who has been able to turn her anger about her own failed marriage into some constructive, domestically ironic revenge, as Alice uses her dead husband's shirts as "dust cloths, monthly rags, rags tied around pipe joints to hinder freezing; pot holders and pieces to test hot irons and wrap their handles."[152] With Alice's action, Violet is able to receive glimpses of the *not-yet-become* for herself.

Violet's crucial turning point occurs when Alice tells her, "You got anything left to you to love, anything at all, do it."[153] The reflection about Alice's command causes the healing to start because when Alice is burning a shirt with her iron shortly afterward, Violet laughs, initially at this burnt shirt, but then she continues to laugh about herself until she has laughed away her anger and frustration. Now equipped with a *tabula rasa*, she is able to regain an ability she owned in her youth but lost when she moved to the northern city. She is able again to love and to accept herself as the woman she really is, not allowing any destructive inferiority complex to whisper to her all the things she does not have but should have to make a man love her. When she finally heals from her complex, she is able to tell about herself:

> ...messed up my life... Forgot it was mine. My life. I just ran up and down the streets wishing I was somebody else.... Now I want to be the

[151] Lucille P. Fultz, "'Slips of Sorrow': Narrating the Pain of Difference and the Rhetoric of Healing," *Toni Morrison. Playing with Difference* (Urbana and Chicago: University of Illinois Press, 2003) 72.

[152] Morrison, *Jazz*, 83.

[153] Morrison, *Jazz*, 112.

> woman my mother didn't stay around long enough to see. That one. The one she would have liked and the one I used to like before.[154]

With her new self-love, she is able to help her husband overcome his own complexes and problems and wins back his love, and both are now able to enjoy the beauty of their relationship of their youth, now adjusted to their older age and their life in the North.

In Walker's *Possessing the Secret of Joy*, Tashi's healing process starts when she moves to Switzerland, where she begins sessions with a psychologist, the Old Man. During her talks with him, she slowly realizes that she herself has to become the agent for her healing. According to Bloch's theory, an important step in the protagonists' development happens when they are granted an epiphany. Tashi's epiphany occurs when the Old Man is showing her pictures and films from his trips to Africa. One of the films includes a village's female initiation ceremony. The pictures show exactly all the scenes Tashi thought she had forgotten such as the row of feet of already circumcised girls and the cock that eats the thrown-away flesh. Suddenly, she understands that her sister Dura did not simply bleed to death because of a play-related accident but died because of her initiation ceremony. Her new knowledge helps her now to complete her spiritual healing process.

Shange's *for colored girls*, Naylor's *Brewster Place*, and McMillan's *Waiting to Exhale* focus on communities of women in which each individual is allowed to go through a healing process and simultaneously serves as a catalyst for the others. In her *for colored girls who have considered suicide*, Shange has all of her women who live alone in their miseries join as a group to experience possible sister support. As Gabbin observes, "They come together and recognize the bonds that have brought them together and the ties that will keep them

---

[154] Morrison, *Jazz*, 208.

close."[155] From now on, every woman will be able to face her problems without running away or getting crushed by them because she knows that she can rely on a community of sisters for support. Such a community of emotional and spiritual support allows the possibility of a healing process of every single one of them.

As the women in *colored girls* serve each other as catalysts while still healing themselves, the women in *Brewster Place* help each other with supporting sisterhood while going through a transforming process. Among the many examples of sisterly support in *Brewster Place*, Mattie's fight for Ciel's survival can stand as the prototype for the idea of supporting sisterhood. When Ciel refuses to participate in life any longer after she aborts a baby she actually wanted very much and in addition loses her other child, a two-year-old daughter, to a fatal accident, Mattie watches the dying Ciel and decides to fight for Ciel's spiritual reaffirmation of life again:

> [Mattie] sat on the edge of the bed and enfolded the tissue-thin body in her huge ebony arms. And she rocked. Ciel's body was so hot it burned Mattie when she first touched her, but she held and rocked.... Mattie rocked her out of that bed, out of that room, into a blue vastness just underneath the sun and above time. She rocked her over Aegean seas so clean they shone like crystal, so clear the fresh blood of sacrificed babies torn from their mothers' arms and given to Neptune could be seen like pink froth on the water. She rocked her on and on, past Dachau, where soul-gutted Jewish mothers swept their children's entrails off laboratory floors. They flew past the spilled brains of Senegalese infants whose mothers had dashed them on the wooden sides of slave ships. And she rocked on.
>
> She rocked her into her childhood and let her see murdered dreams. And she rocked her back, back into the womb, to the nadir of her hurt, and they found it ... it would heal.[156]

In Bambara's *The Salt Eaters*, Velma's mental and physical breakdown was caused by her split spiritual and rational personality. Velma herself realizes one morning, "Something crucial had been missing from the political/ economic

[155] Gabbin, "A Laying On of Hands," 262.

[156] Gloria Naylor, *The Women of Brewster Place* (New York: Penguin Books, 1983) 103.

social/ cultural/ aesthetic/ military/ psychological / psychosocial/ psychosexual mix."[157] Gloria Hull explains that Velma "broke down being solely political and relentlessly logical, and gets well when she comes into conscious possession of her spiritual being."[158] The healing process can take place because during her trance, Velma relives all the past situations that broke her spirit. One more time, she can consider the events and now decide what was wrong, what would be worth preserving, and how she should act differently in the future. During Velma's trance, Minnie Ransom guides her as a soul sister, serving as the catalyst many protagonists in the discussed texts are privileged to have. In the end, Velma concludes her healing process as Maya Angelou's image of the caged but singing bird suggests: Velma awakes from her trance, ready "to shout, to laugh, to sing."[159]

Jones's *Corregidora's* Ursa finally comprehends the whole picture of male abuse in her family; she, too, is able to complete her healing process. Because she finally learns that the true meaning of the maternal tradition of passing on the stories of sexual abuse was not so much to keep historical memories but to pass the hatred of men to the next daughter, Ursa is now able to understand her own problems with men in relationships. She now realizes that her own lack of self-esteem and her insecurities as a woman have contributed to the failure of her marriage, too. As a first step, her new knowledge enables her to understand that she does not have to accept her husband's mental and physical mistreatment.

With this knowledge that empowers her, she resolves to fight against his abuse, using his own methods. For example, since he uses sex as a tool for punishment or reward whenever he feels like doing so, she refuses his advances

---

[157] Bambara, *The Salt Eaters*, 259.

[158] Gloria Hull, "What It Is I Think She's Doing Anyhow: A Reading of Toni Cade Bambara's *The Salt Eaters*," *Home Girls. A Black Feminist Anthology*, ed. Barbara Smith (New York: Kitchen Table-Women of Color Press, 1983) 128.

[159] Bambara, *The Salt Eaters*, 295.

one day and tells him, "I'm just playing it your way. Something else I learned."[160] One incident will become a milestone for her fight for dignity because afterward she considers herself liberated from him. After an evening in a bar where he deliberately and repeatedly embarrasses her in public, she tells him:

> You wont [sic!] to show everybody when we out in public that you got your … piece—but when we here you act like you ain't got shit. I ain't no more than a piece of shit. Well, you got your piece a shit. I can play your games to, buddy. Tomorrow night you can just come on down to the place and sell your piece a shit, cause I don't give a damn.[161]

At this point, Ursa's healing process might at first glance not look like a healing process to some readers because she reconciles with her husband despite the fact that she still hates him. Yet it is a stepping stone into the direction that Ursa still has to learn to be willing to love and accept love, to respect and to accept respect.

The highlight of her healing process happens after their sexual reconciliation. Ursa and Mutt, her husband, have a blues-like dialogue with each other that proves her willingness and her new ability to ask for equality and pay respect to a man, but simultaneously to ask for the same respect and equality from him. When Mutt tells her that he does not want a woman who will hurt him, her response is, "Then you don't want me."[162] He repeats his line of "I don't want a kind of woman that hurt you" several times to her, but her response reminds, "Then you don't want me." Yet, finally, Ursa's answer changes; Jones allows her the following end to their blues dialogue:

> "I don't want a kind of woman that hurt you."
> "Then you don't want me."

---

[160] Jones, *Corregidora*, 157.

[161] Jones, *Corregidora*, 165.

[162] Jones, *Corregidora*, 185.

> He shook me until I fell against him crying. "I don't want a kind of man that'll hurt me neither," I said.[163]

Although the dialogue at the end of Jones's novel presents a very ambivalent closing scene, it still proves that Ursa has moved from victim to victor because, as Cheryl Wall emphasizes, "rather than a beating, the conversation between Ursa and Mutt ends in an embrace."[164]

In Williams's *Dessa Rose*, Ruth, the white woman who hides runaway slaves on her farm, has to learn to correct her self-image of a generous woman whom all Black people would love to befriend and work for. She seriously thinks that the Black people living with her truly love her. For example, she talks repeatedly about her nanny, Dorcas, and the tremendous love Dorcas had for her. Ruth's crisis starts when Dessa Rose, a runaway slave who was able to escape from a slave catcher's jail, tells Ruth that she does not know anything about Black people, not even about her nanny. Dessa makes Ruth aware that she does not even know Dorcas's real name since Ruth has assumed all the time that Dorcas's name was Mammy. Step by step, Dessa forces Ruth to face her invented, convenient image of Dorcas. When Ruth still desperately needs to believe that Dorcas did not have children of her own—"She just had me! I was like her child"[165]—so that in Ruth's imagination Dorcas simply loved Ruth as a mother would, Dessa insists that Dorcas had children of her own. To make her point clear, Dessa explains the reality of slave mothers to Ruth, until this time a situation strangely unknown to Ruth.

By and by, Ruth has to realize that she does not know anything about Dorcas but has all the time created a certain picture of her, using stereotypes and

---

[163] Jones, *Corregidora*, 185.

[164] Wall, *Worrying the Line*, 138.

[165] Sherley Anne Williams, *Dessa Rose* (New York: William Morrow and Company, 1986) 119.

images that slaveholders had of Black people. For instance, in her stories about Dorcas, Ruth always states, "I know Mammy didn't know a thing about history, but I knew she was right about the clothes. She used to dress me so pretty."[166] With her statement, Ruth implies that a Black person does not have enough intelligence to understand the larger society, but to fill this void, gets his or her life's pleasure from serving a white family wholeheartedly.

Ruth's transformation happens when she realizes that she, indeed, does not know anything about Black people and consequently has to start anew in her relationships with them. This time, however, she knows she has to listen to them and consider them as equally important as herself. Even if her transformation implies a long and painful process, she is well on her way at the end of the novel. That the Black people on her farm indeed accept the changing Ruth becomes obvious in their willingness to take Ruth with them on their way to the West.

In a discussion of concrete utopias, I have to call special attention to one text in particular, Toni Morrison's *Paradise*, which has often been called a utopian text. For example, Tom Moylan offers an intriguing reading of *Paradise* as a literary utopia. He shows that the inhabitants of Ruby, a small all-Black town in Oklahoma founded after World War II by a group of Black people who were seeking new homes for their families, start their residential experiment as a traditional utopia with all its "lingering hopes, that surround and inform the utopian impulse for a better way to live in a harsh and unjust world."[167] Yet while most critics stay with the traditional utopian reading, Moylan already shows that *Paradise*'s utopia is more complex; he explains that the original utopian text turns into "a cruel caricature of Utopia that in the course of the novel turns into its own anti-Utopia."[168] In addition to Moylan' reading, I want to suggest that *Paradise* can also be read as a Blochian utopian text. Linda Krumholz's reading of

[166] Williams, *Dessa Rose*, 118.

[167] Tom Moylan, "Introduction: Jameson and Utopia," *Utopian* Studies 9.2 (1998): 2.

[168] Moylan, "Introduction," 2.

Paradise offers an intriguing connection between Moylan's idea of the cruel and anti-utopian caricature and a possible Blochian interpretation when she suggests the following about the text:

> Morrison's novel occurs in "that holy hollow between sighting and following through," [73] as the men take aim [to kill the five women at the convent] but have not yet fired. The text of *Paradise* expands that moment into a space of insight, revision, and grace, a grace period for the reader. The leaping women signify a new point of departure, a leap out of the unknown into new possibilities of representation and imagination.[169]

To illustrate my own Blochian point, I want to look at one inhabitant of *Paradise*, Soane, who serves as a Faustian representative. Morrison portrays Soane, one of the mothers in Ruby, as having a hard time dealing with her everyday life and her mental stability even many years after her two sons' deaths in Vietnam. For the longest time, Soane's only ways to cope with the deaths have been bitterness and confusion. Yet Morrison allows Soane to start a healing process when Soane finally begins to meditate on the complex relationship between racism and personal guilt. Contemplating the death of her two sons, Scout and Easter, Soane realizes how much she has also been guilty of their deaths by being so naïve about Vietnam. Since she had not questioned at all the imperialistic goals of the U.S. government in Vietnam, she had unintentionally, but still actively, supported U.S. imperialism: "How proud and happy she was when they enlisted; she had actively encouraged them to do so. Their father had served in the forties. Uncles too."[170] In her naïveté, Soane indeed had believed that young black men would be safer in Vietnam than in any other American city, "safer in the army than in Chicago where Easter wanted to go. Safer than Birmingham, than Montgomery, Selma, than Watts. Safer than Money, Mississippi in 1955 and Jackson, Mississippi in

---

[169] Linda J. Krumholz, "Reading and Insight in Toni Morrison's *Paradise*," *African American Review* 36.1 (2002): 22.

[170] Toni Morrison, *Paradise* (New York: Alfred A. Knopf, 1998) 100.

1963.... [In Vietnam] her sweet colored boys [would be] unshot, unlynched, unmolested, unimprisoned."[171] But Morrison makes Soane also realize that her naïveté was actually caused by the life-long personal experience of American racism; because of American racist reality, Soane was indeed right to assume that her black teenage boys would be in true danger in any American place. Soane does learn to see and understand the complex connection between racism and personal guilt. By finally admitting personal responsibility and accepting her failure and at the same time recognizing where she has a right to blame America for its racism, Soane is able to find the distance necessary to heal spiritually.

Because Bloch is interested in the changed society, the process of healing should transfer from the protagonists to their immediate surroundings. According to him, a successful personal, spiritual journey should affect the larger community because these two areas influence each other: A miserable personal life is often more or less a result of the way the protagonist lives in a community or the larger society. The texts of the discussed writers meet Bloch at this point, for they, too, see the inseparableness of the personal and the political. As Bloch does, they, too, deal with the nexus between the protagonists' responsibility for personal agency and for societal change. Looking at the connection between the personal and the larger society, the writer Alexis DeVeaux discusses the texts of her peers:

> I see a greater and greater commitment among black women writers to understand self, multiplied in terms of the community, the community multiplied in terms of the nation, and the nation multiplied in terms of the world. You have to understand what your place as an individual is and the place of the person who is close to you. You have to understand the space between you before you can understand more complex and larger groups.[172]

---

[171] Morrison, *Paradise*, 101.

[172] Claudia Tate, "Alexis DeVeaux," *Black Women Writers at Work* (Harpenden, England: Oldcastle Books, 1985) 55.

In my previous chapters, I showed how Bloch's community idea applies to *Beloved*, *Bailey's Café*, and *Daughters of the Dust*. In all of these texts, the protagonists celebrate community in the end. After much struggle, they can see at least fragments of a changed society, and the texts offer enough potential to hope for further transformations. The same celebration of community can also be observed in the texts discussed in this chapter, such as Bambara's *The Salt Eaters*, Naylor's *Brewster Place*, Shange's *for colored girls*, and McMillan's *Waiting to Exhale*. In Shange's and McMillan's texts, transforming women come together and experience each other as community, thus assuring each other that in future times of crisis, they will support each other. In *Brewster Place*, the characters literally celebrate each other by throwing a street party. Even the meanest woman, Eva, whose greatest pleasure has been to badmouth others and to despise every attempt at community, participates and helps with the buffet.

However, the *Brewster* people's celebration of community does not stop with simply dancing and eating together. The highlight that shows a true Blochian community that brings about societal changes occurs when they all come together to destroy the wall that has kept them apart from the rest of the city and has contributed to their self-image of the forgotten underclass in the ghetto. The act of tearing down the wall is highly symbolic in regard to the Blochian idea of politics from below: Nobody will change anything for them if they themselves, the people from Brewster Place, do not begin to fight for transformation.

The Salt Eaters, too, displays its Blochian content in its call for conscious political intervention from below. Bambara's novel indeed presents an excellent example of the Blochian program, of personal responsibility for the future. The novel's main motif— "choices to be noted. Decisions to be made"[173]—aims at the Blochian concept of everybody's responsibility for political actions in his or her own community. To illustrate her point, Bambara offers a dystopian version of the

---

[173] Bambara, *The Salt Eaters*, 274.

future that could exist if people neglected their personal responsibility for politics from below. In her dystopia, one observes the following:

> ...[contaminated bodies] cannot be cremated because of the smoke and the wind and the rain, and can't be buried because missiles would be heated up by the contamination and there is no room anymore underground, space taken up by equipment and uniforms. Bodies that can't be launched into space anymore because ... beings out there are sick of spinning satellites and telstars [sic] and intrusive rocket probes and have made the terms clear.[174]

Despite the dystopian version, *The Salt Eaters* is a novel about hope. To express the hope for her healing community, Bambara employs Velma, the broken and the healing one, as a symbol for the community at large. Elliot Butler-Evans argues about Velma's function as a symbol:

> Her disintegration and fragmentation reflect the "madness" of the community as a whole, and her attempt to move from illness to health (fragmentation to wholeness) represents both a personal process and one in which the larger community is engaged. Her character, then, assumes a complex representational status. In addition to an individual, personal narrative, Velma Henry is a metaphor for a larger story.[175]

Emphasizing the fact that Velma's healing is really the story about the community's transformation, Gloria Hull explains Bambara's stylistic method of depicting the individual and the community in her novel; the story starts with Velma's hospital room, but then, step by step, the story unfolds in ever-widening circles, from Velma's person to "the ring of twelve who hum and pray with Minnie; to the music room cluttered with staff, visitors, and assorted onlookers; to the city of Clayborne surrounding the Infirmary walls; to the overarching sky

---

[174] Bambara, *The Salt Eaters*, 274.

[175] Elliott Butler-Evans, *Race, Gender, and Desire. Narrative Strategies in the Fiction of Toni Cade Bambara, Toni Morrison, and Alice Walker* (Philadelphia: Temple University Press, 1989) 180.

above and the earth beneath.... From the center, the threads web out, holding a place and weaving links between everything and everybody."[176]

However, although the novel ends with Velma's healing, it does not depict a transformed society resulting from a progressive revolution. Philip Page explains that in comparison to many other African American writers whose communities are not as diverse as Bambara's, *The Salt Eaters*' community is so complex, "encompassing individuals, families, communities, American society, and the entire globe and involving psychological, social, economic, political, and environmental dimensions," that the "forces needed for recovery must be eclectic."[177] Still, I claim that even in this regard, *The Salt Eaters* is a Blochian text of societal hope. With such a universal and complex approach, Bambara would not be able to offer a completely transformed community. Yet she meets Bloch in this regard because he claims that the transformed society will not come as a result of a single historical event but because of individuals with constant change-willing attitudes who understand that society will always need transformation; therefore, they will keep working on improving any society's conditions. And Bambara, too, claims in very Blochian terminology in *The Salt Eaters* that the transformation of a community "must be done all over again, all over again, all over again."[178]

Likewise, Morrison does not allow *Paradise* to end with a community that has finally found its peace and healing; her text cannot be called a utopian happy ending at all. But again, Blochian texts do not see the necessity of the perfect place, but rather call for open endings that provide Faustian representatives who are *en route*. And Soane's change lets the reader hope that she will help her

---

[176] Hull, "What It Is I Think She's Doing Anyway," 125.

[177] Philip Page, "Across the Borders: Imagining the Future in Toni Cade Bambara's *The Salt Eaters*," *Reclaiming Community in Contemporary African American Fiction* (Jackson: University Press of Mississippi, 1999) 78.

[178] Bambara, *The Salt Eaters*, 255.

community's members receive glimpses of the *not-yet-become*, too, thus joining Soane and also becoming people *en route*, who one day will stand as "free people on free ground."

In *Possessing the Secret of Joy*, Walker allows a glimpse of an already changing larger female society. After her own spiritual healing, Tashi decides for her own agency and murders Mbati, the village circumciser and a national hero in Tashi's African home country. Even if the novel ends with Tashi's execution, it is still a novel about Blochian hope because at Tashi's execution, many women show their willingness to take over Tashi's fight. In many different ways, these women signal to Tashi during her last minutes that her death will not be in vain because other women will take over her fight against female mutilation and will change conditions for the next female generations.

Perhaps one of the most moving examples of a changed community is expressed in the dialogue between Dessa and Ruth in Williams's *Dessa Rose*. After Ruth learned to not simply create Black people's personalities according to her stereotypes of them but to understand that an equal society is possible only if every side is willing to pay respect in its fullest meaning and not merely as lip service, Dessa, too, is willing to learn to respect Ruth. One can observe their attempt at community with each other after Ruth tricks Dessa out of jail. Instead of addressing each other in the typical slave society's way, they tell each other, "My name Ruth. Ruth, I ain't your mistress … my name Dessa, Dessa Rose. Ain't no O to it…. 'Ruth,' 'Dessa,' we said together."[179]

Their transformed community is still very much a fragmented community because they both realize, "We couldn't hug each other, not on the streets, not in Arcopolis, not even after dark; we both had sense enough to know that. The town could even bar us from laughing; but that night we walked the boardwalk together

---

[179] Williams, *Dessa Rose*, 232.

and we didn't hide our grins."[180] However, it is at least a start of a community that has not existed before in history. Thus, there is hope for a possible society of equality between different races in the future.

Although novels like *Jazz*, *Praisesong for the Widow*, and *Corregidora* do not end with an obvious community celebration as the other novels do, they still carry the Blochian hope content for future societal changes. First, the protagonists will tell others about their transformations, thus inviting more people to reflect about their own possible transformations. For example, as far as *Praisesong* is concerned, Bambara claims in her analysis of Marshall's novel that the new Avatara will not only pass on her knowledge to her grandchildren's generations but, in addition, will assume the task of warning others about the dislocation from one's nation and culture.[181]

Second, these novels do indeed carry Bloch's concrete utopian impulse because the very fact that the protagonists' transformations could take place proves that some patterns of their respective societies have been broken. Therefore, the next generation will already face new conditions that will allow them to focus on necessary changes in their own societies. One can realistically hope that the protagonists will inspire readers, too: to dare to dream ahead, to be willing to have visions, and to risk turning these ideas into future realities.

---

[180] Williams, *Dessa Rose*, 232.

[181] Toni Cade Bambara, "Reading the Signs, Empowering the Eye," *Black American Cinema*, ed. Manthia Diawara (New York: Routledge, 1993) 131.

Conclusion

In his *Keeping Faith*, Cornel West devotes one chapter to his ideas about the "new cultural politics of difference." He explains that his theory of aesthetics deals with art that "reject[s] the abstract, general, and universal in light of the concrete, specific and particular and historicize[s], contextualize[s] and pluralize[s] by highlighting the contingent, provisional, variable, tentative, shifting and changing."[182] In his analysis, West focuses especially on one of the theory's main features, the idea of inspiring recipients of art toward personal agency. West's notion of art meets Bloch's concept of the hope-inspiring concrete utopian theory. West's thoughts can be considered a direct continuation of Bloch's theory. Bloch, too, asks for art that inspires people to turn their daydreams into revolutionary willingness for personal agency.

However, in a world that since Bloch's publication of *The Principle of Hope* has become much more complex and globalized, for many people the idea of politics from below seems to be more and more impossible. West believes

---

[182] Cornel West, "The New Cultural Politics of Difference," *Keeping Faith* (New York: Routledge, 1993) 3.

these doubts arise because "a world in which most of the resources, wealth and power are centered in huge corporations and supportive political elites, the new cultural politics of difference may appear to be sole visionary, utopian and fanciful."[183] Therefore, one might argue that not only West's, but also Bloch's, ideas are too idealistic and do not apply anymore to the early twentieth-first century.

Yet, as Ben Anderson argues as recently as 2006, there has been "renewed interest across the social sciences in the problems and tasks that surround the concept of the utopia and the practice of utopianism. Post critiques that classical 'blueprint' utopianism has been at best eliminative of difference, and at worst authoritarian, recent work has experimented with dynamic, open-ended conceptions of utopia."[184] I already discussed such renewed recent interest in my first chapter where I cited philosophers such as Fredric Jameson and Zygmunt Bauman who argue for the need of utopian concepts such as Bloch's for contemporary societies.

And West, too, does argue that politics from below is not only as necessary as it was at all other times during history, but also that it is even possible. As one example, West cites the revolutions in Eastern Europe and the fall of communism. Even if economic breakdown was a major contributing factor to the fall of the communist system, the people's visions of changed circumstances played the main part in transforming those societies. Regarding the role of art, it is a well-known fact that not only were major intellectuals, among them many writers, the spiritual leaders of these movements, but that art was a widely used tool for inspiring large groups toward visions of changed societies.

Looking at the contemporary African American women writers in particular, as I do, it is therefore possible to apply Bloch's theory to their texts,

---

[183] West, "New Cultural Politics of Difference," 31.

[184] Ben Anderson, "'Transcending without Transcendence': Utopianism and an Ethos of Hope," *Antipode* 38.4 (Sep. 2006): 691.

even many decades after the publication of *The Principle of Hope*. A Blochian application always deals with a specific historical and cultural group, and in the case of the discussed authors, it is clear that they intend to inspire their own, the African American group, toward personal agency. Barbara Christian explains how these texts have already had an impact on African American lives:

> Our vision is still seen, even by many progressives, as secondary, our words trivialized as minority issues or women's complains, our stance sometimes characterized by others as divisive. But there is a deep philosophical reordering that is occurring in this literature that is already having its effects on so many of us whose lives and expressions are an increasing revelation on the *intimate* face of universal struggle.[185]

In *Breaking Bread*, their dialogue about the late twentieth-century situation of African Americans, Cornel West and bell hooks both see the texts of contemporary African American women writers as major tools for overcoming the nihilism that still can be found in the Black community of today, for these texts provide fictitious visions of changed African American characters and communities.[186]

One might argue that the impact of art on politics exists but cannot be a major one since the Eastern European countries did not turn into perfect societies and the current African American community still faces major problems despite the civil rights movements in the 1960s and the changes that have happened in American society since then. However, Bloch explains that many people make the mistake of seeing revolution only as a one-time historical event; they do not understand that the attempt at improving societies must be an ongoing struggle. As Velma learns in *The Salt Eaters* that revolution has to "be done all over again,

---

[185] Barbara Christian, "Creating a Universal Literature: Afro-American Women Writers," *Black Feminist Criticism* (New York: Pergamon Press, 1985) 163.

[186] bell hooks and Cornel West, *Breaking Bread* (Boston: South End Press, 1991) 54-55. See also West's discussion of nihilism in the African American community in: Cornel West, "Nihilism in Black America," *Race Matters* (Boston: Beacon Press, 1993) 9-20.

all over again, all over again,"[187] so emphasizes Bloch, repeatedly, that *revolutionary forward dreaming* has to become an attitude, implying that one has to work constantly on societal changes and can never stop in this process. And art is indeed the medium that will remind people of their constant, never-ending responsibility for personal agency in that it is able to provide its recipients with glimpses of the *not-yet-become*.

As Bloch reminds one with *Faust*, of course, Faust knows that the ultimate moment to which he can, finally, say "Stay awhile, you are so fair" does not exist, yet humans have the responsibility to actively pursue this vision and to strive toward the fulfillment of standing "with free people on free ground." The African American women writers discussed here do fulfill the Blochian requirement of inspiring readers to provide these glimpses of Bloch's concept of the *pre-appearance*, to stand "with free people on free ground," or, to say it with Baby Suggs's words from Morrison's *Beloved*, "to belong to a community of other free Negroes—to love and be loved by them, to counsel and be counseled, to protect and be protected, feed and be fed."[188]

---

[187] Bambara, *The Salt Eaters*, 255.

[188] Morrison, *Beloved*, 217.

Bibliography

Primary Sources: African American Authors

Angelou, Maya. *I Know Why the Caged Bird Sings*. Toronto: Bantam Books, 1971.

Bambara, Toni Cade. *The Salt Eaters*. New York: Vintage Books, 1980.

Dash, Julie. Screenplay. *Daughters of the Dust. The Making of an African American Woman's Film*. New York: The New Press, 1992. 73-164.

_____. *Daughters of the Dust*. New York: Dutton, 1997.

Jones, Gayl. *Corregidora*. Boston: Beacon Press, 1975.

Marshall, Paule. *Praisesong for the Widow*. New York: Penguin Books, 1983.

McMillan, Terry. *Waiting to Exhale*. New York: Pocket Books, 1992.

_____. *Disappearing Acts*. New York: Pocket Books, 1989.

Morrison, Toni. *Beloved*. New York: PLUME, 1988.

_____. "The Bird Is in Your Hands." *Nobel Lectures from the Literature Laureates 1986 to 2006*. Ed. The Nobel Foundation. New York and London: The Free Press, 2007. 182-190.

_____. *Jazz*. New York: Alfred A. Knopf, 1992.

_____. *Paradise*. New York: Alfred A. Knopf, 1998.

Naylor, Gloria. *Bailey's Café*. Thorndike, Maine: G.K. Hall § Co., 1992.

_____. *The Women of Brewster Place*. New York: Penguin Books, 1983.

Shange, Notzake. *For colored girls who have considered suicide when the rainbow is enuf*. New York: Macmillan Publishing Company, 1989.

Walker, Alice. *Possessing the Secret of Joy*. New York: Harcourt Brace Jovanovich Publishers, 1992.

_____. *By the Light of My Father's Smile*. New York: Random House, 1998.

_____. *The Color Purple*. New York: Pocket Books, 1982.

Williams, Sherley Anne. *Dessa Rose*. New York: William Morrow and Company, 1986.

Primary Sources: Ernst Bloch

Bloch, Ernst. *The Utopian Function of Art and Literature. Selected Essays.* Translated by Jack Zipes and Frank Mecklenburg. Cambridge, MA: The MIT Press, 1988.

_____. *Abschied von der Utopie? Vorträge.* Ed. Hanna Gekle. Frankfurt am Main: Suhrkamp, 1980.

_____. *Tendenz, Latenz, Utopie.* Frankfurt am Main: Suhrkamp, 1985.

_____. *Das Prinzip Hoffnung.* 1959. 1st edition. Frankfurt am Main: Suhrkamp, 1985.

_____. *The Principle of Hope.* Translated by Neville Plaice, Stephen Plaice and Paul Knight. Cambridge, MA: The MIT Press, 1986.

_____. *Heritage of Our Times.* Translated by Neville Plaice and Stephen Plaice. Cambridge, UK: Polity Press, 1991.

_____. *Literary Essays.* Translated by Andrew Joran and others. Stanford, CA: Stanford University Press, 1998.

_____. *The Spirit of Utopia.* Translated by Anthony A. Nassar. Stanford, CA: Stanford University Press, 2000.

_____. "Man as Possibility." *Cross Currents* (Summer 1968): 273-283.

_____. "Die Welt bis zur Kenntlichkeit verändern." *Tagträume vom aufrechten Gang. Sechs Interviews mit Ernst Bloch.* Ed. Arno Münster. Frankfurt am Main: Suhrkamp, 1977. 20-100.

_____. "Ein Marxist hat nicht das Recht, Pessimist zu sein." *Tagträume vom aufrechten Gang. Sechs Interviews mit Ernst Bloch.* Ed. Arno Münster. Frankfurt am Main: Suhrkamp, 1977. 101-120.

_____. *Viele Kammern im Welthaus. Eine Auswahl aus dem Werk.* Eds. Friedrich Dieckmann and Jürgen Teller. Frankfurt am Main: Suhrkamp, 1994.

Bloch, Ernst and Theodor W. Adorno. "'Something's Missing': A Discussion between Ernst Bloch and Theodor W. Adorno on the Contradiction of Utopian Longing (1964)." *The Utopian Function of Art and Literature. Selected Essays.* Cambridge, MA: The MIT Press, 1988. 1-18.

Bloch, Ernst, Theodor W. Adorno, Walter Benjamin, Bertolt Brecht, Georg Lukács. *Aesthetics and Politics.* Afterword by Fredric Jameson. London and New York: Verso, 1977.

Secondary Sources: Ernst Bloch

Anderson, Ben. "'Transcending without Transcendence': Utopianism and an Ethos of Hope." *Antipode* 38.4 (Sep. 2006): 691-710.

_____. "A Principle of Hope: Recorded Music, Listening Practices and the Immanence of Utopia." *Geografiska Annaler Series B: Human Geography* 84.3/4 (2002): 211-228.

Arnold, Heinz Ludwig, ed. *Ernst Bloch*. München: Edition Text + Kritik, 1985.

Bahr, Erhard. "The Literature of Hope: Ernst Bloch's Philosophy and Its Impact on the Literature of the German Democratic Republic." *Fiction and Drama in Eastern and Southeastern Europe*. Eds. Henrik Birnbaum and Thomas Eekman. Columbus, OH: Slavica Publishers, 1980. 11-26.

Bauman, Zygmunt. "To Hope Is Human." *TIKKUN* 19.6 (2004): 64-67.

_____. "Utopia with no Topos." *History of the Human Sciences* 16.1 (2003): 11-26.

Benzaquen, Adriana S. "Thought and Utopia in the Writings of Adorno, Horkheimer, and Benjamin." *Utopian Studies* 9.2 (1998): 149-162.

Bodei, Remo. "Darf man noch hoffen?" *Verdinglichung und Utopie. Ernst Bloch und Georg Lukács zum 100. Geburtstag*. Eds. Arno Münster, Michael Löwy, and Nicolas Tertulian. Frankfurt am Main: Sendler, 1987. 206-218.

Bothner, Roland. *Die Materie, die Kunst und der Tod. Studien zu Ernst Bloch aus den Jahren 1986 bis 2006*. Heidelberg: Edition Publish & Parish, 2006.

_____. *Kunst im System. Die konstruktive Funktion der Kunst für Ernst Blochs Philosophie*. Bonn: Bouvier, 1983.

Braun, Bruce. "Writing Geographies of Hope." *Antipode* 37.4 (2005): 834-841.

Braun, Eberhard. "'...und worin noch niemand war: Heimat': Zum Finale furioso von Blochs *Prinzip Hoffnung*." *Bloch-Almanach 8*. Ludwigshafen: Ernst-Bloch-Archiv, 1988.

_____. "Antizipation des Seins wie Utopie: Zur Grundlegung der Ontologie des Noch-Nicht-Seins im *Prinzip Hoffnung*." *Seminar zur Philosophie Ernst Blochs*. Ed. Burghart Schmidt. Frankfurt am Main: Suhrkamp, 1983.

Brenner, Peter. "Kunst als Vor-Schein: Blochs Ästhetik und ihre ontologischen Voraussetzungen." *Literarische Utopieentwürfe*. Ed. Hiltrud Gnüg. Frankfurt am Main: Suhrkamp, 1982. 39-52.

Browne, Craig. "Hope, Critique, and Utopia." *Critical Horizons* 6 (2005): 63-86.

Crapanzano, Vincent. "Reflections on Hope as a Category of Social and Psychological Analysis." *Cultural Anthropology* 18.1 (Feb. 2003): 3-32.

Czajka, Anna. *Poetik und Ästhetik des Augenblicks. Studien zu einer neuen Literaturauffassung auf der Grundlage von Ernst Blochs literarischem und literaturästhetischem Werk*. Berlin: Duncker & Humblot, 2006.

Daniel, Jamie Owen, and Tom Moylan, eds. *Not Yet! Reconsidering Ernst Bloch*. London and New York: Verso, 1997.

Daniel, Jamie Owen. "Warm Thought: Reassessing Bloch's Aesthetics." *Utopian Studies* 1.2 (1990): 85-95.

Focke, Wenda. *Etüden I. Über Freiheit, Hoffnung und Bewußtsein. Gedanken zu Jean Améry und Ernst Bloch*. Cuxhaven: Junghans Verlag, 1990.

Gardiner, Michael E. "Marxism and the Convergence of Utopia and the Everyday." *History of the Human Sciences* 19.3 (2006): 1-32.

Gekle, Hanna. "The Phenomenology of the Wish in *The Principle of Hope*." *New German Critique* 45 (1988): 55-69.

_____. Afterword. *Abschied von der Utopie? Vorträge*. Ernst Bloch. Ed. Hanna Gekle. edition suhrkamp 104. Frankfurt am Main: Suhrkamp, 1980. 217-239.

_____. *Wunsch und Wirklichkeit: Blochs Philosophie des Noch-Nicht-Bewussten und Freuds Theorie des Unbewussten*. Frankfurt am Main: Suhrkamp, 1986.

Geoghegan, Vincent. "Ideology and Utopia." *Journal of Political Ideologies* 9.2 (June 2004):123-138.

_____. "Remembering the Future." *Not Yet! Reconsidering Ernst Bloch*. Eds. Jamie Owen Daniel and Tom Moylan. London: Verso, 1997. 15-32.

_____. "Utopia, Religion and Memory." *Journal of Political Ideologies* 12.3 (Oct. 2007): 255-267.

_____. *Ernst Bloch*. London and New York: Routledge, 1996.

Giroux, Henry A. "When Hope Is Subversive." *TIKKUN* 19.6 (Nov. 2004): 62-64.

Gross, David. "Ernst Bloch and the Dialectics of Hope." *The Unknown Dimension*. Eds. Dick Howard and Karl E. Klare. New York: Basic Books, 1972. 107-130.

Gunn, Richard. "Ernst Bloch's *The Principle of Hope*." New Edinburgh Review 76 (1987): 90-98.

Habermas, Jürgen. "Ernst Bloch: Ein marxistischer Schelling." *Philosophisch-politische Profile*. Frankfurt am Main: Suhrkamp, 1981.

Hansen, Horst. *Die Kopernikanische Wende in die Ästhetik. Ernst Bloch und der Geist seiner Zeit*. Würzburg: Königshausen § Neumann, 1998.

Hedges, Inez. "Faust and Utopia: Socialist Visions." *Socialism & Democracy* 13.1 (Spring/Summer 1999): 47-73.

_____. *Framing Faust. Twentieth-Century Cultural Struggles*. Carbondale, IL: Southern Illinois University Press, 2005.

Heubrock, Dietmar. *Utopie und Lebensstil. Eine empirische Untersuchung zur Bedeutung von Ernst Blochs Konzept der "konkreten Utopie" für eine materialistisch-psychologische Utopieforschung*. Köln: Pahl-Rugenstein, 1988.

Holländer, Hans. "Der Bildcharakter des 'Vor-Scheins', auch in der Sprache." *Materialien zu Ernst Blochs Prinzip Hoffnung*. Ed. Burghart Schmidt. edition suhrkamp 111. Frankfurt am Main: Suhrkamp, 1978. 439-445.

Holz, Hans Heinz. *Logos spermatikos. Ernst Blochs Philosophie der unfertigen Welt*. Darmstadt und Neuwied: Luchterhand, 1975.

Horster, Detlef. *Bloch zur Einführung*. Hamburg: Edition SOAK im Junius Verlag, 1987.

Hudson, Wayne. *The Marxist Philosophy of Ernst Bloch*. London: Macmillan, 1982.

_____. *The Marxist Philosophy of Ernst Bloch*. New York: St. Martin's Press, 1982.

Jameson, Fredric. "Progress versus Utopia; or, Can We Imagine the Future?" *Science Fiction Studies* 9.2 (July 1982): 147-158.

_____. "The Politics of Utopia." *New Left Review* 25 (2004): 35-54.

_____. *Marxism and Form. Twentieth-Century Dialectical Theories of Literature*. Princeton: Princeton University Press, 1971.

Jones, Calvin N. *Negation and Utopia. The German Volksstück from Raimund to Kroetz*. New York: Peter Lang, 1993.

Jung, Werner. "The Early Aesthetic Theories of Bloch and Lukács." *New German Critique* (Fall 1988): 41-54.

Kellner, Douglas, and Harry O'Hara. "Utopia and Marxism in Ernst Bloch." *New German Critique* (Fall 1976): 11-34.

Kessler, Achim. *Ernst Blochs Ästhetik. Fragment, Montage, Metapher*. Würzburg: Königshausen & Neumann, 2006.

Kirchner, Verena. *Im Bann der Utopie*. Heidelberg: Universitätsverlag C. Winter, 2002.

Korngiebel, Wilfried. *Bloch und die Zeichen. Symboltheorie, kulturelle Gegenhegemonie und philosophischer Interdiskurs*. Würzburg: Königshausen & Neumann, 1999.

Kufeld, Klaus, and Peter Zudeick, eds. *"Utopien haben einen Fahrplan". Gestaltungsräume für eine zukunftsfähige Praxis*. Mössingen-Talheim: Talheimer, 2000.

Kufeld, Klaus, and Volker Hörner, eds. *Utopien heute? Zukunftsszenarien für Künste und Gesellschaft*. Heidelberg: Edition Braus, 2002.

Lehmann, Günther Kurt. *Ästhetik der Utopie. Arthur Schopenhauer, Sören Kierkegaard, Georg Simmel, Max Weber, Ernst Bloch*. Stuttgart: Neske, 1995.

Levitas, Ruth. "Educated Hope: Ernst Bloch on Abstract and Concrete Utopia." *Utopian Studies* 1.2 (1990): 13-26.

_____. "For Utopia: The (Limits of the) Utopian Function in Late Capitalist Society." *The Philosophy of Utopia*. Ed. Barbara Goodwin. London: Frank Cass, 2001. 25-43.

_____. Introduction: The Elusive Idea of Utopia. *History of the Human Sciences* 16.1 (2003): 1-10.

Levy, Ze'ev. "Utopia and Reality in the Philosophy of Ernst Bloch." *Utopian Studies* 1.2 (1990): 3-12.

Manuel, Frank. *Utopias and Utopian Thought*. Boston: Houghton Mifflin Company, 1966.

Marzocchi, Virginio. "Utopie als 'Novum' und 'letzte Wiederholung' bei Ernst Bloch." *Ernst Bloch. Text und Kritik*. Ed. Heinz Ludwig Arnold. Special Edition. München: edition text + kritik gmbh, 1985. 194-207.

Maucher, Andreas. *Die Rettung des Fortschritts. Ernst Bloch im "Diskurs der Moderne"*. Konstanz: Hartung-Gorre, 1989.

McManus, Susan. "Fabricating the Future: Becoming Bloch's Utopians." *Utopian Studies* 14.2 (2003): 1-22.

_____. "Theorizing Utopian Agency: Two Steps toward Utopian Techniques of the Self." *Theory & Event* 10.3 (2007): 10.

Morris-Keitel, Peter. Rev. of *Im Bann der Utopie*, by Verena Kirchner. *Utopian Studies* 15.1 (2004): 130-131.

Moylan, Tom. "Bloch against Bloch: The Theological Reception of *Das Prinzip Hoffnung* and the Liberation of the Utopian Function." *Not Yet! Reconsidering Ernst Bloch*. Eds. Jamie Owen Daniel and Tom Moylan. London: Verso, 1997. 96-121.

_____. "The Locus of Hope: Utopia versus Ideology." *Science-Fiction Studies* 9 (1982): 159-166.

Münster, Arno, Michael Löwy, and Nicolas Tertulian, eds. *Verdinglichung und Utopie. Ernst Bloch und Georg Lukács zum 100. Geburtstag*. Frankfurt am Main: Sendler, 1987.

_____. *Tagträume vom aufrechten Gang. Sechs Interviews mit Ernst Bloch.* Frankfurt am Main: Suhrkamp, 1977.

Münz-Koenen, Ingeborg. *Konstruktion des Nirgendwo. Die Diskursivität des Utopischen bei Bloch, Adorno, Habermas*. Berlin: Akademie Verlag, 1997.

Nordquist, Joan. *Ernst Bloch*. Santa Cruz, CA: Reference and Research Services, 1990.

Plaice, Neville, Stephen Plaice, and Paul Knight. Translators' Introduction. *The Principle of Hope*. Ernst Bloch. Oxford: Basil Blackwell, 1986. xix-xxxiii.

Riedel, Manfred. *Tradition und Utopie. Ernst Blochs Philosophie im Licht unserer geschichtlichen Denkerfahrung.* Frankfurt am Main: Suhrkamp, 1994.

Roberts, Richard H. *Hope and Its Hieroglyph. A Critical Decipherment of Ernst Bloch's Principle of Hope.* Atlanta, GA: Scholars Press, 1990.

Rohrbacher, Klaus. *"Das Hoffen lernen": Ernst Blochs Beiträge zur Pädagogik.* Heidelberg: [s.n.], 1988.

_____, ed. *Zugänge zur Philosophie Ernst Blochs*. Frankfurt am Main: Dipa-Verlag, 1995.

Rorty, Richard. "Hope and the Future." *Peace Review* 14.2 (June 2002): 149-155.

Saage, Richard. *Das Ende der politischen Utopie?* Frankfurt am Main: Suhrkamp, 1990.

Schiller, Hans-Ernst. *Bloch-Konstellationen. Utopien der Philosophie.* Lüneburg: Dietrich zu Klampen, 1991.

Schmidt, Burghart. "Utopie ist keine Literaturgattung." *Literatur ist Utopie*. Ed. Gert Ueding. edition suhrkamp 935. Frankfurt am Main: Suhrkamp, 1978. 17-44.

_____. *Ernst Bloch*. Stuttgart: J.B. Metzler, 1985.

_____. *Kritik der reinen Utopie. Eine sozialphilosophische Untersuchung.* Stuttgart: Metzler, 1988.

_____. ed. *Seminar zur Philosophie Ernst Blochs*. Frankfurt am Main: Suhrkamp, 1983.

Schmidt, Denis J. "Kunst, Kritik und die Sprache der Philosophie: Zum Beitrag Blochs." *Philosophische Rundschau* 34 (1987): 299-305.

Shor, Francis. "Utopian Aspirations in the Black Freedom Movement: SNCC and the Struggle for Civil Rights, 1960-1965." *Utopian Studies* 15.2 (2004): 173-189.

Skrimshire, Stefan. "Another What is Possible? Ideology and Utopian Imagination in Anti-Capitalist Resistance." *Political Theology* 7.2(2006): 201-219.

Solnit, Rebecca. *Hope in the Dark. Untold Histories, Wild Possibilities*. London: New Left Books, 2004.

Steiner, George. "Träume nach vorwärts." *Materialien zu Ernst Blochs Prinzip Hoffnung*. Ed. Burghart Schmidt. edition suhrkamp 111. Frankfurt am Main: Suhrkamp, 1978. 195-200.

Tassone, Giuseppe. "The Politics of Metaphysics: Adorno and Bloch on Utopia and Immortality." *European Legacy* 9.3 (2004): 357-367.

Ueding, Gert, ed. "Blochs Ästhetik des Vorscheins." *Ästhetik des Vorscheins*. Ernst Bloch. Frankfurt am Main: Suhrkamp, 1974. 7-27.

_____. "Das Fragment als literarische Form der Utopie." *Etudes Germaniques* 41:3 (1986): 351-362.

_____. "Ernst Blochs Philosophie der Utopie." *Utopieforschung. Interdisziplinäre Studien zur neuzeitlichen Utopie*. Ed. Wilhelm Voßkamp. Stuttgart: Metzler, 1982. 293-303.

_____. "Literatur ist Utopie." *Literatur ist Utopie*. Ed. Gert Ueding. edition suhrkamp 935 . Frankfurt am Main: Suhrkamp, 1978. 7-14.

_____. "Schein und Vorschein in der Kunst. Zur Ästhetik Ernst Blochs." *Materialien zu Ernst Blochs Prinzip Hoffnung*. Ed. Burghart Schmidt. edition suhrkamp 111. Frankfurt am Main: Suhrkamp, 1978. 446-463.

Ujma, Christina. *Ernst Blochs Konstruktion der Moderne aus Messianismus und Marxismus. Erörterungen mit Berücksichtigung von Lukács und Benjamin*. Stuttgart: M & P, 1995.

Vidal, Francesca, ed. *"Kann Hoffnung enttäuscht werden?"* Mössingen-Talheim: Talheimer, 1998.

_____. *Kunst als Vermittlung von Welterfahrung. Zur Rekonstruktion der Ästhetik von Ernst Bloch*. Würzburg: Königshausen § Neumann, 1994.

Waterworth, Jayne. *A Philosophical Analysis of Hope*. London: Palgrave, 2003.

Webb, Darren. "Modes of Hoping." *History of the Human Sciences* 20.3 (August 2007): 65-83.

Zimmermann, Rainer E., and Gerd Koch, eds. *U-Topoi. Ästhetik und politische Praxis bei Ernst Bloch*. Mössingen-Talheim: Talheimer Verlag, 1996.

Zimmermann, Rainer E. *Subjekt und Existenz. Zur Systematik Blochscher Philosophie*. Berlin: Philo, 2001.

Zournazi, Mary, ed. *Hope. New Philosophies for Change*. Sydney: Pluto Press, 2002.

Zubke, Friedhelm. "'Der Ton geht mit uns...': Die Utopie der Musik." *Bloch-Almanach 21*. Ludwigshafen: Ernst-Bloch-Archiv, 2002.

_____. "Hoffen und den Frieden träumen! Der Hoffnungsbegriff bei Ernst Bloch und Erich Fromm." *Bloch-Almanach 14*. Ludwigshafen: Ernst-Bloch-Archiv, 1995. 69-92.

Secondary Sources: Ernst Bloch--Related Studies

Adorno, Theodor W. *Aesthetics and Politics*. London: Verso, 2007.

Ashcroft, Bill. "Critical Utopias." *Textual Practice* 21.3 (2007): 411-431.

Brown, Nicholas. *Utopian Generations. The Political Horizon of Twentieth-Century Literature.* Princeton: Princeton University Press, 2005.

Buchanan, Ian. "Metacommentary on Utopia, or Jameson's Dialectic of Hope." *Utopian Studies* 9.2 (1998): 18-30.

Erzgräber, Willi. *Utopie und Anti-Utopie*. München: Wilhelm Fink Verlag, 1980.

Fitting, Peter. "The Concept of Utopia in the Work of Fredric Jameson." *Utopian Studies* 9.2 (1998): 8-17.

Harvey, David. *Spaces of Hope*. Berkeley: University of California Press, 2000.

Jucker, Rolf, ed. *Zeitgenössische Utopieentwürfe in Literatur und Gesellschaft. Zur Kontroverse seit den achtziger Jahren.* Amsterdam and Atlanta, GA: Rodopi, 1997.

Leopold, David. "Socialism and (the Rejection of) Utopia." *Journal of Political Ideologies* 12.3 (2007): 219-237.

Manuel, Frank. *Utopias and Utopian Thought.* Boston: Houghton Mifflin Company, 1966.

Moylan, Tom. "Special Section on the Work of Fredric Jameson." *Utopian Studies* 9.2 (1998): 1-7.

Niezen, Ronald. "Postcolonialism and the Utopian Imagination." *Israel Affairs* 13.4 (2007): 714-729.

Oizerman, T.I. "Introduction to Marxism and Utopianism." *Russian Studies in Philosophy* 44.2 (Fall 2005): 5-23.

Ruppert, Peter. *Reader in a Strange Land. The Activity of Reading Literary Utopias*. Athens: University of Georgia Press, 1986.

Von Boeckmann, Staci L. "Marxism, Morality, and the Politics of Desire: Utopianism in Fredric Jameson's *The Political Unconscious*." *Utopian Studies* 9.2 (1998): 31-50.

Voßkamp, Wilhelm, ed. *Utopieforschung. Interdisziplinäre Studien zur neuzeitlichen Utopie*. Stuttgart: Metzler, 1982.

Webb, Darren. *Marx, Marxism and Utopia*. Burlington: Ashgate, 2000.

Secondary Sources: Utopian Studies and Feminism

Bammer, Angelika. *Partial Visions. Feminism and Utopianism in the 1970s*. New York and London: Routledge, 1991.

Barr, Marleen, and Nicholas D. Smith, eds. *Women and Utopia. Critical Interpretations*. Lanham: University Press of America, 1983.

Curtis, Claire P. "Rehabilitating Utopia: Feminist Science Fiction and Finding the Ideal." *Contemporary Justice Review* 8.2 (2005): 147-162.

Dietze, Gabriele. *Die Überwindung der Sprachlosigkeit. Texte aus der Neuen Frauenbewegung*. Darmstadt/Neuwied: Luchterhand, 1979.

Holland-Cunz, Barbara, ed. *Feministische Utopien. Aufbruch in die post-patriarchale Gesellschaft*. Meitingen: Corian-Verlag, 1986.

Johnson, Greg. "The Situated Self and Utopian Thinking." *Hypatia* 17.3 (2002): 21-46.

Klarer, Mario. *Frau und Utopie. Feministische Literaturtheorie und Utopischer Diskurs im Anglo-Amerikanischen Roman*. Darmstadt: Wissenschaftliche Buchgesellschaft, 1993.

McKenna, Erin. *The Task of Utopia. A Pragmatist and Feminist Perspective*. Lanham, MD: Rowman & Littlefield Publishers, 2001.

Mellor, Anne K. "On Feminist Utopias." *Women's Studies* 9.3 (1982): 241-263.

Rohrlich, Ruby, and Elaine Hoffman Baruch, eds. *Women in Search of Utopia. Mavericks and Mythmakers*. New York: Schocken Books, 1984.

Tagliacozzo, Sara. "Utopias of Change." *European Journal of Women's Studies* 11.3 (2004): 381-396.

Welter, Barbara. "The Cult of True Womanhood: 1820-1860." *American Quarterly* 18 (1966): 151-174.

Secondary Sources: African American Literature--General

Abernathy, Jeff. *To Hell and Back. Race and Betrayal in the Southern Novel*. Athens, GA: University of Georgia Press, 2003.

Awkward, Michael. *Inspiring Influences. Tradition, Revision, and Afro-American Women's Novels*. New York: Columbia University Press, 1989.

Baker, Houston A., Jr. *Workings of the Spirit. The Poetics of Afro-American Women's Writing*. Chicago: University of Chicago Press, 1991.

Brown-Guillory, Elizabeth, ed. *Middle Passages and the Healing Place of History. Migration and Identity in Black Women's Literature*. Columbus: Ohio State University Press, 2006.

Boesenberg, Eva. *Gender, Voice, Vernacular. The Formation of Female Subjectivity in Zora Neale Hurston, Toni Morrison and Alice Walker*. Heidelberg: Universitätsverlag C. Winter, 1999.

Busia, Abena P.A. "What is Your Nation? Reconnecting Africa and Her Diaspora through Paule Marshall's *Praisesong for the Widow*." *Changing Our Own Words*. Ed. Cheryl Wall. New Brunswick and London: Rutgers University Press, 1989. 196-212.

Butler-Evans, Elliott. *Race, Gender, and Desire. Narrative Strategies in the Fiction of Toni Cade Bambara, Toni Morrison, and Alice Walker*. Philadelphia: Temple University Press, 1989.

Byerman, Keith E. "'Dear Everything': Alice Walker's *The Color Purple* as Womanist Utopia." *Utopian Thought in American Literature*. Eds. Arno Heller, Walter Hölbing, and Waldemar Zacharasiewicz. Buchreihe zu den Arbeiten aus Anglistik und Amerikanistik 1. Tübingen: Gunter Narr, 1988. 171-183.

Caruth, Cathy. Introduction. *Psychoanalysis, Culture and Trauma*. Ed. Cathy Caruth. Special Issue of *American Imago* 48.1 (1991): 1-12.

Chinosole, [no first name]. "Audre Lorde and Matrilineal Diaspora: Moving History beyond Nightmare into Structures for the Future." *Wild Women in the Whirlwind. Afra-American Culture and the Contemporary Literary Renaissance*. Eds. Joanne M. Braxton and Andree Nicola McLaughlin. New Brunswick: Rutgers University Press, 1990. 379-394.

Christian, Barbara. "'Somebody Forgot to Tell': African American Women's Historical Novels." *Wild Women in the Whirlwind. Afra-American Culture and the Contemporary Literary Renaissance*. Eds. Joanne M. Braxton and Andree Nicola McLaughlin. New Brunswick: Rutgers University Press, 1990. 326-341.

_____. "But What Do We Think We're Doing Anyway: The State of Black Feminist Criticism(s) or My Version of a Little Bit of History." *Within the Circle. An Anthology of African American Literary Criticism from the Harlem Renaissance to the Present*. Ed. Angelyn Mitchell. Durham and London: Duke University Press, 1994. 499-514.

_____. "Creating a Universal Literature: Afro-American Women Writers." *Black Feminist Criticism*. New York: Pergamon Press, 1985. 159-163.

_____. "Literature since 1970." *African-American Literature. The Norton Anthology*. Eds.Henry Louis Gates, Jr. and Nellie Y. McKay. New York: W.W. Norton, 1997. 2011-2020.

_____. "The Race for Theory." *Within the Circle. An Anthology of African American Literary Criticism from the Harlem Renaissance to the Present*. Ed. Angelyn Mitchell. Durham and London: Duke University Press, 1994. 348-359.

_____. "Trajectories of Self-Definition: Placing Contemporary Afro-American Women's Fiction." *Black Feminist Criticism*. New York: Pergamon Press, 1985. 171-186.

Cotton, Angela L., and Christa Davis Acampora, eds. *Cultural Sites of Critical Insight. Philosophy, Aesthetics, and African American and Native*

American Women's Writings. Albany, NY: State University of New York Press, 2007.

Cowan, Rosemary. *Cornel West. The Politics of Redemption.* Cambridge, UK: Blackwell, 2003.

Davis, Amanda J. "To Build a Nation: Black Women Writers, Black Nationalism, and the Violent Reduction of Wholeness." *Frontiers: A Journal of Women Studies* 26.3 (2005): 24-53.

Elsley, Judy. "'Nothing can be sole or whole that has not been rent': Fragmentation in the *Quilt* and *The Color Purple*." *Critical Essays on Alice Walker*. Ed. Ikenna Dieke. Westport: Greenwood Press, 1999. 163-170.

Evans, James H. *Spiritual Empowerment in Afro-American Literature. Frederick Douglass, Rebecca Jackson, Booker T. Washington, Richard Wright, Toni Morrison*. Lewiston, NY: The Edwin Mellen Press, 1987.

Fannin, Alice. "A Sense of Wonder: The Pattern for Psychic Survival in *Their Eyes Were Watching God* and *The Color Purple*." *Zora Neale Hurston Forum* 1 (1986): 1-11.

Gabbin, Joanne V. "A Laying On of Hands: Black Women Writers Exploring the Roots of Their Folk and Cultural Tradition." *Wild Women in the Whirlwind. Afra-American Culture and the Contemporary Literary Renaissance*. Eds. Joanne M. Braxton and Andree Nicola McLaughlin. New Brunswick: Rutgers University Press, 1990. 246-263.

Gates, Henry Louis, Jr. *Figures in Black. Words, Signs, and the "Racial" Self.* New York: Oxford University Press, 1987.

_____. *The Signifying Monkey*. New York: Oxford University Press, 1988.

Griffin, Farah Jasmine. "Toni Cade Bambara: Free to Be Anywhere in the Universe." *Callaloo* 19.2 (1996): 229-231.

Guillaumin, Colette. "The Masculine: Denotations/Connotations." *Feminist Issues* 5 (1985): 65-73.

Henderson, Mae. "'Where, by the Way, Is this Train Going?': A Case for Black (Cultural) Studies." *Postcolonial Theory and the United States. Race, Ethnicity, and Literature*. Eds. Amritjit Singh and Peter Schmidt. Jackson: University Press of Mississippi, 2000. 95-102.

_____. "Speaking in Tongues: Dialogics, Dialectics, and the Black Woman Writer's Literary Tradition." *Changing Our Own Words*. Ed. Cheryl Wall. New Brunswick and London: Rutgers University Press, 1989. 16-34.

Holloway, Karla. "Revision and (Re)membrance: A Theory of Literary Structures in Literature by African-American Women Writers." (1990). *The Prentice Hall Anthology of African American Women's Writers*. Ed. Valerie Lee. Upper Saddle River, NJ: Pearson, 2006. 405-411.

Holmes, Linda Janet, and Cheryl A. Wall, eds. *Savoring the Salt. The Legacy of Toni Cade Bambara.* Philadelphia, PA: Temple University Press, 2007.

hooks, bell, and Cornel West. *Breaking Bread. Insurgent Black Intellectual Life.* Boston: South End Press, 1991.

hooks, bell. *Black Looks. Race and Representation.* Boston: South End Press, 1992.

_____. "Reading and Resistance: *The Color Purple.*" *Alice Walker. Critical Perspectives Past and Present.* Amistad Literary Series. Eds. Henry Louis Gates, Jr. and K.A. Appiah. New York: Amistad, 1993. 284-295.

Hull, Gloria. "What It Is I Think She's Doing Anyhow: A Reading of Toni Cade Bambara's *The Salt Eaters.*" *Home Girls. A Black Feminist Anthology.* Ed. Barbara Smith. New York: Kitchen Table-Women of Color Press, 1983. 124-144.

Jones, L. Gregory. "Some Kind of Tomorrow." *Christian Century* 118.8 (2001): 22.

Kelley, Margot Anne. "'Damballah is the first law of thermodynamics': Modes of Access to Toni Cade Bambara's *The Salt Eaters.*" *African American Review* 27.3 (1993): 479-493.

_____. "Sisters' Choices: Quilting Aesthetics in Contemporary African-American Women's Fiction." *Quilt Culture. Tracing the Pattern.* Ed. Cheryl B. Torsney and Judy Elsley. Columbia: University of Missouri Press, 1994. 167-194.

Kelley, Robin D.G. *Freedom Dreams. The Black Radical Imagination.* Boston: Beacon Press, 2002.

Koenen, Anne. *Zeitgenössische afro-amerikanische Frauenliteratur. Selbstbild und Identität bei Toni Morrison, Alice Walker, Toni Cade Bambara und Gayl Jones.* Frankfurt and New York: Campus Verlag, 1985.

Lee, Valerie, ed. *The Prentice Hall Anthology of African American Women's Writers.* Upper Saddle River, NJ: Pearson, 2006.

McDowell, Deborah E. "'The Changing Same': Generational Connections and Black Women Novelists." *Reading Black, Reading Feminist.* Ed. Henry Louis Gates, Jr. New York: Meridian Book, 1990. 91-115.

_____. "New Directions for Black Feminist Criticism." (1980). *Within the Circle. An Anthology of African American Literary Criticism from the Harlem Renaissance to the Present.* Ed. Angelyn Mitchell. Durham and London: Duke University Press, 1994. 428-441.

_____. "Transferences: Black Feminist Thinking: The 'Practice' of 'Theory.'" *The Changing Same. Black Women's Literature, Criticism, and Theory.* Bloomington and Indianapolis: Indiana University Press, 1995. 156-176.

Mills, Fiona, and Keith Mitchell, eds. *After the Pain. Critical Essays on Gayl Jones.* New York: Peter Lang, 2006.

Moore, Opal. "Building an Edifice of Hope and Human Possibility." *Black Issues in Higher Education* 14.14 (4 Sep. 1997): 28-29.

Morrison, Toni. Preface. *Deep Sighting and Rescue Missions. Fictions, Essays, and Conversations.* Toni Cade Bambara. New York: Pantheon Books, 1996. vii-xi.

Page, Philip. "Across the Borders: Imagining the Future in Toni Cade Bambara's *The Salt Eaters.*" *Reclaiming Community in Contemporary African American Fiction*. Jackson: University Press of Mississippi, 1999. 78-115.

Parker-Smith, Bettye J. "Alice Walker's Women: In Search of Some Peace of Mind." *Black Women Writers (1950-1980)*. Ed. Mari Evans. New York: Anchor Press, 1984. 478-492.

Quashie, Kevin Everod. *Black Women, Identity, and Cultural Theory. (Un)becoming the Subject.* New Brunswick, N.J.: Rutgers University Press, 2004.

Ramadanovic, Petar. "When '*to die in freedom*' Is Written in English: Cathy Caruth's *Unclaimed Experience.*" *Forgetting Futures. On Memory, Trauma, and Identity*. Lanham: Lexington Books, 2001. 81-96.

Reid, Shelley E. "Beyond Morrison and Walker: Looking Good and Looking Forward in Contemporary Black Women Stories." *African American Review* 34.2 (2000): 313-328.

Russell, Sandi. *Render Me My Song. African-American Women Writers from Slavery to the Present*. New York: St. Martin's Press, 1990.

Sample, Maxine. "Walker's *Possessing the Secret of Joy.*" *Explicator* 58.3 (2000): 169-173.

Shor, Francis. "Utopian Aspirations in the Black Freedom Movement: SNCC and the Struggle for Civil Rights, 1960-1965." *Utopian Studies* 15.2 (2004): 173-189.

_____. Rev. of *Freedom Dreams. The Black Radical Imagination*, by Robin D.G. Kelley. *Utopian Studies* 15.1 (2004): 128-129.

Simcikova, Karla. *To Love, Fully, Here and Now. The Healing Vision in the Works of Alice Walker*. Lanham: Lexington Books, 2007.

Smith, Barbara. "Toward a Black Feminist Criticism." (1977). *Within the Circle. An Anthology of African American Literary Criticism from the Harlem Renaissance to the Present*. Ed. Angelyn Mitchell. Durham and London: Duke University Press, 1994. 410-427.

Spaulding, A. Timothy. *Re-forming the Past. History, the Fantastic, and the Postmodern Slave Narrative.* Columbus: Ohio State University Press, 2005.

Tate, Claudia. "Alexis DeVeaux." *Black Women Writers at Work*. Harpenden, England: Oldcastle Books, 1985. 49-59.

Wall, Cheryl A., ed. *Changing Our Own Words. Essays on Criticism, Theory, and Writing by Black Women*. New Brunswick and London: Rutgers University Press, 1989.

_____. *Worrying the Line. Black Women Writers, Lineage, and Literary Tradition.* Chapel Hill: University of North Carolina Press, 2005.

Wenker, Stefanie. *Alice Walkers Romanwerk. Eine Untersuchung zu Ganzheit(lichkeit) und Womanism*. Frankfurt am Main and New York: Peter Lang, 2000.

West, Cornel. "Nihilism in Black America." *Race Matters*. Boston: Beacon Press, 1993. 9-20.

_____. "The Crisis of Black Leadership." *Race Matters*. Boston: Beacon Press, 1993. 3-32.

_____. "The New Cultural Politics of Difference." *Keeping Faith*. New York: Routledge, 1993. 3-32.

Wilentz, Gay Alden. *Healing Narratives. Women Writers Curing Cultural Disease*. New Brunswick: Rutgers University Press, 2000.

Willis, Susan. *Specifying. Black Women Writing the American Experience*. Madison: University of Wisconsin Press, 1987.

Secondary Source: Toni Morrison

Atwood, Margaret. "Haunted by Their Nightmares." Rev. of *Beloved*, by Toni Morrison. *New York Times*, 13 September 1987, 48-50.

Bell, Bernard W. "*Beloved*: A Womanist Neo-Slave Narrative; or Multivocal Remembrances of Things Past." *Critical Essays on Toni Morrison's Beloved*. Ed. Barbara H. Solomon. New York: G.K. Hall, 1998. 166-176.

Boesenberg, Eva. *Gender, Voice, Vernacular. The Formation of Female Subjectivity in Zora Neale Hurston, Toni Morrison and Alice Walker*. Heidelberg: Universitätsverlag C. Winter, 1999.

Boudreau, Kristin. "Pain and the Unmaking of Self in Toni Morrison's *Beloved*." *Understanding Toni Morrison's Beloved and Sula*. Eds. Solomon O. Iyasere and Marla W. Iyasere. Troy, NY: Whitston Publishing Company, 2000. 258-276.

Bouson, J. Brooks. *Quiet as It's Kept. Shame, Trauma and Race in the Novels of Toni Morrison*. New York: State University of New York Press, 2000.

Bröck, Sabine. "Postmodern Mediations and *Beloved*'s Testimony: Memory Is Not Innocent." *Amerikastudien/American Studies* 43.1 (1998): 33-49.

Daniels, Jean. "The Call of Baby Suggs in *Beloved*: Imagining Freedom in Resistance and Struggle." *Griot: Official Journal of the Southern Conference on Afro-American Studies* 21.2 (Fall 2002): 1-7.

DeKoven, Marianne. "Postmodernism and Post-Utopian Desire in Toni Morrison and E. L. Doctorow." *Toni Morrison. Critical and Theoretical Approaches*. Ed. Nancy Peterson. Baltimore, MD: Johns Hopkins University Press, 1997. 111-130.

Fultz, Lucille P. "'Slips of Sorrow': Narrating the Pain of Difference and the Rhetoric of Healing." *Toni Morrison. Playing with Difference*. Urbana and Chicago: University of Illinois Press, 2003. 46-76.

Jablon, Madelyn. "Rememory, Dream Memory, and Revision in Toni Morrison's *Beloved* and Alice Walker's *The Temple of My Familiar*." *CLA Journal* 37.2 (1993): 136-144.

Joyner, Louisa. *Toni Morrison. Beloved, Jazz, Paradise*. London: Vintage, 2003.

Krumholz, Linda J. "Reading and Insight in Toni Morrison's *Paradise.*" *African American Review* 36.1 (2002): 21-34.

Kubitschek, Missy Dehn. *Toni Morrison. A Critical Companion.* Westport: Greenwood Press, 1998.

LeClair, Thomas. "'The Language Must Not Sweat': A Conversation with Toni Morrison." *Toni Morrison. Critical Perspectives Past and Present.* Eds. Henry Louis Gates, Jr. and K.A. Appiah. New York: Amistad, 1993. 369-377.

Michael, Magali Cornier. "Re-imagining Agency: Toni Morrison's *Paradise.*" *African American Review* 36.4 (2002): 643-662.

Morrison, Toni, and Cornel West. "Blues, Love and Politics." *Nation* 278.20 (24 May 2004): 18-28.

Morrison, Toni. "Rootedness: The Ancestor as Foundation." *Black Women Writers (1950-1980).* Ed. Mari Evans. New York: Anchor Books, 1984. 339-345.

Norton, Furaha DeMar. "On Trauma, Self-Knowledge, and Resilience: History and the Ethics of Selfhood in Toni Morrison's *Beloved, Jazz,* and *Paradise.*" *Dissertation Abstracts International, Section A: The Humanities and Social Sciences* 62.12 (June 2002): 4169.

Page, Philip. "Traces of Derrida in Toni Morrison's *Jazz.*" *African American Review* 29.1 (1995): 55-66.

_____. *Dangerous Freedom. Fusion and Fragmentation in Toni Morrison's Novels.* Jackson: University Press of Mississippi, 1996.

Powell, Betty Jane. "'Will the parts hold?' The Journey toward a Coherent Self in *Beloved.*" *Understanding Toni Morrison's Beloved and Sula.* Eds. Solomon O. Iyasere and Marla W. Iyasere. Troy, NY: Whitston Publishing Company, 2000. 143-154.

Ramadanovic, Petar. "In the Future: Reading for Trauma in Toni Morrison's *Beloved.*" *Forgetting Futures. On Memory, Trauma, and Identity.* Lanham: Lexington Books, 2001. 97-120.

Rand, Naomi R. *Silko, Morrison, and Roth. Studies in Survival.* New York: Peter Lang, 1999.

_____. "Surviving What Haunts You: The Art of Invisibility in *Ceremony, The Ghost Writer* and *Beloved.*" *MELUS* 20.3 (Fall 1995): 21-32.

Raphael-Hernandez, Heike. "A Journey to Independence: Toni Morrison's *Beloved* and the Critical Utopia." *Flips Sides. New Critical Essays in American Literature.* Ed. Klaus H. Schmidt. Frankfurt am Main: Peter Lang, 1995. 43-60.

Raynaud, Claudine. "*Beloved* or the Shifting Shapes of Memory." *The Cambridge Companion to Toni Morrison.* Ed. Justine Tally. Cambridge: Cambridge University Press, 2007. 43-58.

Romero, Channette. "Creating the Beloved Community: Religion, Race, and Nation in Toni Morrison's *Paradise.*" *African American Review* 39.3 (2005): 415-430.

Tally, Justine. Introduction: "All necks are on the line." *The Cambridge Companion to Toni Morrison.* Ed. Justine Tally. Cambridge: Cambridge University Press, 2007. 1-7.

Tate, Claudia. "Toni Morrison." *Black Women Writers at Work.* Harpenden, England: Oldcastle Books, 1985. 117-131.

Timothy, Ellen L. "Individuation and the Paradox of Love: Toni Morrison's Pedagogy of Transformation and Healing." *Dissertation Abstracts International, Section A: The Humanities and Social Sciences* 65.11 (May 2005): 4144.

Wolter, Jürgen C. "'Let People Know Where Their Power Is': Deconstruction and Re-Membering in Toni Morrison's *Beloved.*" *Zeitschrift für Anglistik und Amerikanistik: A Quarterly of Language, Literature and Culture* 45.3 (1997): 236-246.

Secondary Source: Gloria Naylor

Brantley, Jenny. "Women's Screams and Women's Laughter: Connections and Creations in Gloria Naylor's Novels." *Gloria Naylor's Earlier Novels.* Ed. Margot Anne Kelley. Gainesville, FL: University Press of Florida, 1999. 21-38.

Felton, Sharon, and Michelle C. Loris, eds. *The Critical Response to Gloria Naylor.* Westport, CT: Greenwood, 1997.

_____. "The Human Spirit is a Kick-Ass Thing." *Conversations with Gloria Naylor.* Ed. Maxine Lavon Montgomery. Jackson: University Press of Mississippi, 2004. 138-150.

Fowler, Karen Joy. Rev. of *Baileys Café*, by Gloria Naylor. *Gloria Naylor. Critical Perspectives Past and Present.* Eds. Henry Louis Gates, Jr. and K.A. Appiah. New York: Amistad, 1993. 26-28.

Fowler, Virginia C. *Gloria Naylor. In Search of Sanctuary.* New York: Twayne, 1996.

_____. "A Conversation with Gloria Naylor." *Conversations with Gloria Naylor.* Ed. Maxine Lavon Montgomery. Jackson: University Press of Mississippi, 2004. 123-137.

Gottfried, Amy. "Angry Arts: Silence, Speech, and Song in Gayl Jones's *Corregidora.*" *African American Review* 28.4. (1994): 559-570.

Kelley, Margot Anne. "Framing the Possibilities. Collective Agency and the Novels of Gloria Naylor." *Gloria Naylor's Earlier Novels.* Ed. Margot Anne Kelley. Gainesville, FL: University Press of Florida, 1999. 133-154.

Montgomery, Maxine Lavon, ed. *Conversations with Gloria Naylor.* Jackson: University Press of Mississippi, 2004.

_____. "Authority, Multivocality, and the New World Order in Gloria Naylor's *Bailey's Café.*" *African American Review* 29.1 (1995): 27-34.

Nash, William R. "The Dream Defined: *Bailey's Café* and the Reconstruction of American Cultural Identities." *The Critical Response to Gloria Naylor.* Eds. Sharon Felton and Michelle C. Loris. Westport, CT: Greenwood, 1997. 211-224.

Page, Philip. "Listening below the Surface: Beyond the Boundaries in Gloria Naylor's Fiction." *Reclaiming Community in Contemporary African American Fiction.* Jackson: University Press of Mississippi, 1999. 157-190.

_____. "Living with the Abyss in Gloria Naylor's *Bailey's Café.*" CLA Journal 40.1 (1996): 21-45.

Schneider, Karen. "Gloria Naylor's Poetics of Emancipation: (E)merging (Im)possibilities in *Bailey's Café.*" *Gloria Naylor's Earlier Novels.* Ed. Margot Anne Kelley. Gainesville, FL: University Press of Florida, 1999. 1-20.

Stave, Shirley A., ed. *Gloria Naylor. Strategy and Technique, Magic and Myth.* Newark: University of Delaware Press, 2001.

Whitt, Margaret E. *Understanding Gloria Naylor.* Columbia: University of South Carolina Press, 1999.

Wilson, Charles E. *Gloria Naylor. A Critical Companion.* Westport: Greenwood Press, 2001.

Wood, Rebecca S. "'Two Warring Ideals in One Dark Body': Universalism and Nationalism in Gloria Naylor's *Bailey's Café.*" *African American Review* 30.3 (Fall 1996): 381-395.

Secondary Source: Julie Dash

Bambara, Toni Cade. "Reading the Signs, Empowering the Eye." *Black American Cinema.* Ed. Manthia Diawara. New York: Routledge, 1993. 118-144.

Brouwer, Joel R. "Repositioning: Center and Margin in Julie Dash's *Daughters of the Dust.*" *African American Review* 29.1 (1995): 5-16.

Dash, Julie. "Dialogue between bell hooks and Julie Dash." *Daughters of the Dust. The Making of an African American Woman's Film.* New York: The New Press, 1992. 27-68.

Diawara, Manthia. "Black American Cinema: The New Realism." *Black American Cinema.* Ed. Manthia Diawara. New York: Routledge, 1993. 3-25.

Goodwine, Marquetta L., and The Clarity Press Gullah Project, eds. *The Legacy of Ibo Landing. Gullah Roots of African American Culture.* Atlanta: Clarity, 1998.

Jones, Jacquie. "The Black South in Contemporary Film." *African American Review* 27.1 (1993): 19-24.

Kaplan, Sara Clarke. "Souls at the Crossroads, Africans on the Water: The Politics of Diasporic Melancholia." *Callaloo* 30.2 (2007): 511-526.

McKoy, Sheila Smith. "The Limbo Contest: Diaspora Temporality and Its Reflection in *Praisesong for the Widow* and *Daughters of the Dust*." *Callaloo* 22.1 (1999): 208-222.

Ogunleye, Foluke. "Transcending the 'Dust': African American Filmmakers Preserving the 'Glimpse of the Eternal.'" *College Literature* 34.1 (2007): 156-173.

Tate, Greg. "A Word." *Daughters of the Dust. The Making of an African American Woman's Film*. Julie Dash. New York: The New Press, 1992. 69-72.

Index